Prices and Consumer Information

Prices and Consumer Information

The Benefits from Posting Retail Gasoline Prices

Alex Maurizi
Thom Kelly

American Enterprise Institute for Public Policy Research
Washington, D.C.

Alex Maurizi is a research scientist with Battelle Memorial Institute in Seattle. Thom Kelly is an economist with the Energy Resources Conservation and Development Commission in Sacramento.

Soc
HD
9579
G5
U548

Library of Congress Cataloging in Publication Data

Maurizi, Alex.
    Prices and consumer information.

    (AEI studies ; 193)
    Includes bibliographical references.
        1. Gasoline—Price—United States.   2. Price policy.
    3. Consumer education.   I. Kelly, Thom, joint author.
    II. Title.   III. Series: American Enterprise Institute
    for Public Policy Research. AEI studies ; 193.
    HD9579.G5U548   338.4'3665'538270973   78-8581
    ISBN 0-8447-3295-8

AEI studies 193

Printed in the United States of America

CONTENTS

FOREWORD

This study was conceived nearly five years ago. Two years ago, the undertaking was made possible by the financial assistance of the American Enterprise Institute in purchasing and analyzing the data and by the assistance of Thom Kelly, who had developed the mathematics of a new approach to consumer search theory. The study benefited from the helpful advice and suggestions of several reviewers; specific acknowledgment is in order for the help and guidance provided by David Tuerck, whose careful attention immeasurably improved the analysis and the presentation of the results. Accountability for the analysis and any flaws in it remains, of course, with me, since I was responsible for the overview and the empirical analysis presented in chapters 1 and 3 and Appendix B, and with Thom Kelly, who was responsible for the new approach to consumer search presented in chapter 2 and Appendix A.

ALEX MAURIZI

1
POLICY ISSUES

The question whether advertising makes consumers better off or worse off has become a matter of considerable dispute. Some argue that advertising provides useful information to consumers about the prices and attributes of goods available for purchase. Others argue that advertising raises costs and, therefore, consumer prices without yielding commensurately large benefits in exchange. Some even argue that, besides raising costs, advertising misinforms consumers and in so doing further reduces consumer welfare. To some extent the dispute is an argument over the meaning of the word "advertising," making the controversy more apparent than real. This study seeks to shed some light on this controversy by focusing attention on one type of advertising, namely the advertising of price, and on a theory of consumer behavior according to which price advertising may result in reduced prices by permitting consumers to search more efficiently for low prices. Data on retail gasoline prices and on retail gasoline price posting (the practice of displaying prices on large signs at the station) are examined for evidence of the effects of price advertising and of any link that may exist between these effects and manufacturers' advertising.

Evidence that Advertising Reduces Consumer Welfare

In one of the most comprehensive studies of advertising that has been conducted, William Comanor and Thomas Wilson explored the theory that existing firms use advertising to build brand loyalty and, concomitantly, to create barriers to entry by new firms. Comanor and Wilson argued that, in industries where advertising expenditures are particularly heavy (more than 4 to 5 percent of total firm sales), there are significant excess social costs ascribable to advertising. Such industries exhibit profit rates 3 to 4 percentage points above other industry profit rates. Comanor and Wilson further offered evidence that relative advertising expenditures are more important than relative prices in affecting sales among various industries. Advertising was found to have a major impact on consumer spending.[1]

Comanor and Wilson recognized that consumers can obtain information in a variety of ways, including personal inspection, experience, word of mouth, and such publications as *Consumer Reports*, as well as advertising. The degree to which consumers rely on advertising as a primary information source depends on how costly a means of obtaining information it is relative to other sources. The higher the cost of obtaining information from other sources, the more consumers will rely on advertising.

According to Comanor and Wilson, new entrants to an industry are forced to incur some combination of costs ascribable to price discounting and advertising in order to counter the consumer's familiarity with heavily advertised products of established firms and the consumer's ignorance of products offered by new entrants. The more that existing firms have been able to increase consumer familiarity with their products through advertising, the greater the price discounts new entrants will be forced to offer and the greater the advertising expenses they will be forced to incur in order to win customers.[2]

Comanor and Wilson argued that new entrants suffer an especially severe disadvantage as a result of economies of scale in advertising. Quantity discounts to advertisers and the existence of some level of advertising below which consumers will not recognize a product cause the cost of generating an additional dollar of sales through advertising to fall as sales rise. This permits firms that are able to carve out large market shares through advertising to enjoy lower advertising costs per unit sold than do smaller firms. As an example, Comanor and Wilson cite General Motors and Ford, which from 1954 to 1957 spent only twenty-seven dollars per auto on national advertising while Studebaker and American Motors spent over fifty-eight dollars.[3]

Heavy advertising, then, is said to discourage firms from entering an industry by making it more costly for them to get the attention of consumers than it is for existing firms to keep that attention. The result is that large existing firms can increase profits by raising prices,

---

[1] William S. Comanor and Thomas A. Wilson, *Advertising and Market Power* (Cambridge, Mass.: Harvard University Press, 1974), pp. xi, xii, 239-50.
[2] Ibid., pp. 27-35, 47.
[3] Ibid., pp. 51-53.

knowing that additional firms will not enter and that smaller existing firms will find it hard to compete. The cost to consumers in some industries where advertising is heavy is estimated to be as high as 16 percent of the industry's value added.[4]

A counterargument holds that advertising offers net benefits to consumers in the form of valuable information. When consumers are deprived of this information by prohibitions or restrictions on advertising, the market is made less competitive and consumer prices are increased. This argument is based on the idea that consumers conduct a certain amount of search before making a purchase and that advertising makes search less difficult for the consumer. Instead of increasing excess profits, it is argued, advertising may reduce excess profits by making the market more competitive.

Evidence that Advertising Increases Consumer Welfare

Evidence of the price-reducing effects of advertising has recently been drawn from the prescription drug and retail eyeglass industries. The Federal Trade Commission conducted staff investigations and public hearings on the advisability of eliminating certain retail advertising prohibitions in both industries.[5] John Cady studied the retail prescription drug industry, and Lee and Alexandra Benham studied the eyeglass industry. [6] Each found several hundred million dollars annually in benefits from reduced consumer prices attributable to advertising. Reduced prescription drug prices have been attributed to price advertising, while reduced eyeglass prices have been attributed to both price and nonprice advertising.

---

[4] Ibid., pp. 130-32. See also William S. Comanor and Thomas A. Wilson, "Advertising, Consumer Behavior and Market Imperfections: A Review," Working Paper in Economics No. 88 (Santa Barbara: University of California, September 1977).

[5] Federal Trade Commission, *Prescription Drug Price Disclosures*, Staff Report to the Federal Trade Commission, 1976; Bureau of Consumer Protection, Federal Trade Commission, *Ophthalmic Goods and Services*, Staff Report to the Federal Trade Commission and Proposed Trade Regulation Rule, January 1976; Federal Trade Commission, *Report of the Presiding Officer on Proposed Trade Regulation Rule Regarding Advertising of Ophthalmic Goods and Services*, December 10, 1976.

[6] John Cady, *Restricted Advertising and Competition: The Case of Retail Drugs* (Washington, D.C.: American Enterprise Institute, March 1976); Lee Benham, "The Effect of Advertising on the Price of Eyeglasses," *Journal of Law and Economics*, vol. 15 (October 1972), pp. 337-51, reprinted in *Advertising, Competition, and the Price of Eyeglasses* (Washington, D.C.: American Enterprise Institute, October 1975); Lee Benham and Alexandra Benham, "Regulating through Professions: A Perspective on Information Control," *Journal of Law and Economics*, vol. 18 (October 1975), pp. 421-47.

Retail Drugs. Cady examined state restrictions on the price advertising of retail prescription drugs. He found that in 1970 retail prescription drug prices were over 5 percent higher in states that restricted retail prescription drug price advertising than they were in states that did not. The excess consumer cost attributable to the restrictions was estimated to be from $134 million to $152 million. Given a 150 percent increase in drug sales since 1970, the current annual cost is estimated to be from $336 million to $380 million. Moreover, the lower prices prevailing in states with no advertising restrictions were accompanied by the same level of credit, delivery, and prescription waiting-area services and a higher level of emergency services. Although the monitoring of family prescriptions was provided at a higher level in states that restricted advertising, this service was seen as a way for pharmacies to reduce competition by building customer loyalty. Thus the allowance of price advertising is expected to yield a significant cost saving without bringing about any significant reduction in the overall level of service.[7]

Eyeglasses. The staff of the Federal Trade Commission found that there are numerous legal and private restraints on the freedom of optometrists, ophthalmologists, and opticians to advertise prices or the quality of their services. At both the manufacturing and the wholesaling levels, where price information is readily available, the relative dispersion of prices is small in comparison with that at the retail level.[8] Price and nonprice advertising restrictions were found by Benham to increase retail eyeglass prices by 20 to 100 percent.[9] Since at least half of the more than $1.8 billion spent by consumers nationally on eyeglasses in 1974 was spent in states with price advertising restrictions, those restrictions were found to have increased consumer costs annually by an amount between $180 million and $450 million.[10] This excess consumer cost did not appear to have brought about any offsetting public health or safety benefits. None of the restrictions giving rise to it were found essential to the prevention of false and deceptive advertising; other state and federal laws were found to provide adequate safeguards against such practices. Nor did such

---

[7] Cady, *Advertising.* The Supreme Court has declared unconstitutional certain state restrictions on the advertising of prescription drug prices; see Virginia State Board of Pharmacy v. Virginia Citizens Consumer Council, 425 U.S. 748, 48 L Ed 2d 346 (1976).

[8] Federal Trade Commission, *Advertising of Ophthalmic Goods and Services,* pp. 13-34, 43-45.

[9] Benham, "Effect of Advertising," p. 344.

[10] FTC, *Advertising of Ophthalmic Goods and Services,* p. 49.

4

restrictions appear to have increased the competence of eye care practitioners or the quality of eye examination or eyeglass fabrication. More direct and effective means of quality control were available and in use.[11] The high prices brought about by advertising restrictions were found to have reduced the number of eyeglasses purchased. The Benhams found a 17 to 35 percent decline in the number of eyeglasses purchased, the extent of the decline varying with the degree to which prices were increased.[12]

The Benhams were unable to standardize for either the quality of the eyeglass sold or the quality of the eye examination itself. (Although Cady attempted to account for differences in the nature and frequency of services provided by pharmacies, he did not attempt to measure the quality of prescriptions, that is, whether prescriptions were correctly filled.) Delia Schletter investigated the quality of eyeglass examinations by conducting a controlled test of a sample of eye doctors. Although she found variations in the prescriptions provided, she was informed by one school of ophthalmology that the variations were within acceptable limits. She found no association between the quality of the examination and either the price charged or the firm's decision whether or not to advertise price.[13]

More recently, retired persons in Florida were surveyed concerning their response to optical firms that advertised eyeglass prices (Florida repealed the ban on optician price advertising in July 1976).[14] The firms that advertised prices were found to have a significantly higher proportion of repeat sales than the firms that did not. On the assumption that customer satisfaction provides an indication of quality, this implies that firms that advertise prices offer higher quality per unit of price than firms that do not.

Finally, a recent study done for the California Department of Consumer Affairs found that consumers can expect to find lower prices for the same quality eyewear if they shop around. Firms that advertised other than in the telephone book (whether or not price was advertised) were found to have significanctly lower prices after adjusting for other important factors, such as the quality of the product and whether the firm provided consumers with price information

---

[11] Ibid., pp. 57-72.

[12] Benham and Benham, "Regulating through Professions," pp. 439-40.

[13] Delia N. Schletter, *Optical Illusion* (San Francisco: San Francisco Consumer Action, 1976).

[14] Douglas B. Campbell, "Attitudes of the NRTA-AARP Florida Members toward Eyeglass Purchase and Advertising," (Washington, D.C.: Planning and Research Department, National Retired Teachers Association, American Association of Retired Persons, May 1977).

over the phone about other than the examination price. If consumers in California were to use the guidelines developed by the study, it was estimated that they could probably save between $34.8 million and $54.0 million annually and still obtain the same quality eyewear.[15]

Manufacturers' Advertising Effects Reexamined. Stanley Ornstein recently examined the argument that manufacturers' advertising increases concentration, creates entry barriers, and leads to collusion and monopoly.[16] He concluded that, although a significant, positive relationship exists between advertising and concentration, this relationship is weak and probably a "statistical artifact" traceable to the importance of large firms as heavy advertisers. He further concluded that his findings offered little support to the brand-loyalty or economies-of-scale hypothesis and that they were consistent with the hypothesis (1) that advertising is a means of entry and (2) that firms tend to substitute advertising competition for price competition as they grow large.[17]

Suppose, despite Ornstein's findings, that manufacturers' advertising gave rise to entry barriers and higher manufacturing prices. Would it then also result in higher consumer prices? A recent investigation by Robert Steiner concluded that even if manufacturing prices are raised as a result of manufacturers' advertising, consumer or retail prices might be reduced.[18] This follows not merely as a result of the production economies of scale, whose exploitation is made more profitable by national advertising, but also as a result of a more rapid turnover of nationally advertised products, which brings about a fall in retail profit margins and prices. The lower markup of the advertised products results from an increase in product recognition on the part of consumers that, in turn, makes comparison shopping easier and, hence, increases price competition among retailers. The identifiability of advertised products, Steiner argued, causes the

---

[15] Alex Maurizi et al., *An Economic Analysis of the Regulatory Impact of Selected Boards, Bureaus and Commissions,* a report to the Director of the California Department of Consumer Affairs, November 1977, pp. 203-354.

[16] Stanley I. Ornstein, *Industrial Concentration and Advertising Intensity* (Washington, D.C.: American Enterprise Institute, 1977).

[17] Ibid., p. 11.

[18] Robert L. Steiner, "Does Advertising Lower Consumer Prices?" *Journal of Marketing,* vol. 37 (October 1973), pp. 19-26, reprinted by American Enterprise Institute, Reprint No. 37, January 1976. See also, Robert L. Steiner, *Brand Advertising and the Consumer Goods Economy* (Washington, D.C.: American Enterprise Institute, forthcoming).

retailer to reduce his markups on advertised products in order to avoid a reputation for generally charging higher prices than his competitors.

Finally, the competition from advertised products results in lower prices for similar unadvertised products. Steiner supports his theory with evidence from the toy industry. In 1971, the 100 toys with the largest Christmas sales in the United States had a 25 percent markup, while poorer sellers had a 42 percent markup. Over the period 1971–1972, the 10 toys with the largest Christmas sales in Chicago had a 20 to 20.5 percent markup. Canadian toys that were heavily advertised on television had 20 percent markups in Canada in 1972 while other non-televised Canadian toys had 46 percent markups. Finally, the markup on unadvertised toys in the same category as the heavily advertised toys was as much as 5 to 10 percentage points lower than the markup on unadvertised toys in other categories.[19]

Focus of This Study

This study attempts to estimate the consumer benefits from the posting of retail gasoline prices and to explore the relationship between those benefits and, on the one hand, price posting by gasoline retailers and, on the other, advertising by gasoline manufacturers. Gasoline is a relatively homogenous, easily identifiable product, and retail gasoline price posting is a form of retail price advertising. By examining data on retail gasoline prices and on the frequency of retail gasoline price posting, a measure of the effects on consumer prices of retail price advertising is obtained. By examining data on major-brand retail prices and the frequency of retail price posting among major-brand stations a separate measure of the effects of manufacturers' advertising is obtained. Knowledge of these effects should not only shed some light on the extent to which consumers benefit from price advertising (which increases their search efficiency); it should also shed some light on the extent to which consumers benefit from manufacturers' advertising (which may also increase their search efficiency). Knowledge of both of these effects should narrow the dispute concerning the link between retail prices and manufacturers' efforts to build brand-name identification through advertising. Although the results are only suggestive in this regard, they do appear to shed some additional light upon the relation between manufacturers' advertising and consumer prices.

---

[19] Ibid., pp. 24-25.

Before proceeding to the examination of gasoline prices, this study will explore an extension of conventional demand theory to account for the time consumers spend searching for low prices. This theory, which is presented diagrammatically in chapter 2 and developed mathematically in Appendix A, has implications for the effects on consumer welfare of increases in search efficiency brought about by advertising. Chapter 3 provides the empirical analysis, and chapter 4 offers some policy conclusions.

2

A NEW APPROACH TO CONSUMER SEARCH

Consumer demand theory is ordinarily viewed as a problem in constrained optimization: the individual consumer seeks to maximize utility subject to his budget constraint. Consumers are assumed to face market-determined prices, the knowledge of which is freely available. Although this assumption yields meaningful predictions about economic behavior, it is contradicted by the fact that, because different retailers offer identical goods at different prices, consumers can search rewardingly for price information. By learning more about commodity prices, consumers can save money or increase the volume of goods consumed by paying lower prices per good.

George Stigler has modified consumer demand theory to incorporate the search for price information.[1] In his model, the consumer in search of low prices may canvass many suppliers and only then purchase commodities in the light of additional information. Jacob Mincer, in extending Stigler's analysis to account for the effects of wage changes on search, concludes that the returns to search must equal the opportunity cost of the time invested in search, that is, the wage rate.[2] Generally, the returns to search consist of the additional dollars' worth of goods (including intangible "goods" such as leisure) that the consumer can buy by finding a lower price. These returns are roughly equal to the product of the reduction in price and the number of units of the lower-priced good that the consumer buys before he discovers the lower price. This chapter explores a theory

---

[1] George J. Stigler, "The Economics of Information," *Journal of Political Economy*, vol. 49, no. 3 (June 1961), pp. 213-25.

[2] Jacob Mincer, "Market Prices, Opportunity Costs, and Income Effects," in *Measurement in Economics*, ed. C. F. Christ (Stanford, Calif.: Stanford University Press, 1963).

of price search in a demand-for-leisure framework that treats search as an alternative to work and leisure.

According to standard economic theory, the consumer maximizes utility by increasing consumption of each commodity until the return to spending an additional dollar on that commodity is no greater than the return to spending an additional dollar on any other. The price of leisure is the return obtained through the next best alternative, work, and the return to work is the wage rate. Thus the consumer views leisure as any other commodity, taking more of it until it yields a return no greater than the wage rate. In our framework, there is still another alternative to work—search for more information about lower prices.

By spending a greater proportion of time working, the consumer will increase his income and hence increase the quantity of goods he can purchase, thereby gaining satisfaction. But in order to work more he must either search less, thus decreasing the quantity of goods he can purchase, or decrease his leisure time, or both. In any case, the effect will be to increase his utility somewhat by increasing his earnings and to decrease his utility somewhat by sacrificing leisure or purchasing power. How does the consumer maximize utility in this framework? The solution is to engage in each alternative (work, leisure, or price search) until the return from the last increment of each is no greater than the return from the last increment of any other. Consumers work and rest as well as buy goods; our framework shows that they also take time to search for better buys. The true cost of goods is composed of not only the dollar cost but also the value of the consumer's time spent in search. Since the wage rate measures the price of an hour's time, it also provides a good measure of the cost of search.

Diagrammatic Analysis

To date there has been no contribution to the theory of price search in consumer behavior that analyzes diagrammatically the consumer's price search alternative in comparison with the consumer's work and leisure alternatives. The purpose of this section is to derive the graphical analysis of the consumer's allocation of time among the alternatives of work, leisure, and search.

Consider the price search function depicted in Figure 1. Final commodity price is measured on the vertical axis; the amount of search time is measured on the horizontal axis. The y-intercept (at p_0)

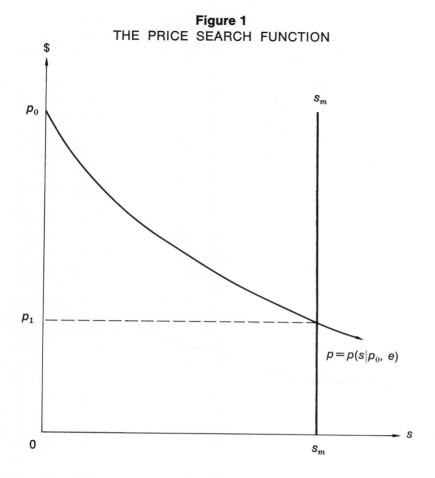

Figure 1
THE PRICE SEARCH FUNCTION

is the price the consumer expects to pay if he buys the commodity without first searching for a lower price. However, since p_0 is the lowest price the consumer knows about at the first of this time period, he believes he can find lower prices if he just invests the time to do so. The price search curve [$p = p(s|p_0)$] is negatively sloped to represent the proposition that as the consumer spends more time in price search he is able to find sellers who quote successively lower prices, for the slope is the reduction in price for a marginal unit of search time. The curve of the price search function becomes horizontal at some positive price, since it is assumed that consumers expect that suppliers have some positive price as the lowest they can offer and still cover short-run costs. (However, the curve is assumed to be continuously decreasing in the relevant range.) [3] The curve is convex to the origin, since it is assumed that as more searches are undertaken each price reduction is smaller than the price reduction just previously found. The minimum expected price from a random sample of searches decreases at a decreasing rate as the number of searches increases.

The distance $0s_m$ represents the total amount of search that the individual can spend if he spends the entire amount of his time (work time plus discretionary time exclusive of subsistence time) searching for lower prices. The vertical line $s_m s_m$ shows this time constraint for all values of initial prices. If this particular consumer elected to spend all his time ($0s_m$) searching, he would determine that the lowest price he could find is p_1. The time invested in search would yield the price reduction $p_0 p_1$ as the total price return to search.

In order to present the remainder of the graphical analysis more readily, it is necessary first to use the conventional graphical analysis for work-leisure choices. In Figure 2, leisure is measured from the left along the horizontal axis and work from the right. Goods are measured on the vertical axis. $x_m l_m$ is the usual linear budget constraint between goods and leisure. If point A is the utility maximizing point for the consumer, $0l_1$ leisure and $0x_1$ goods will be consumed. (Of course, $l_m l_1$ hours of work will be undertaken to buy $0x_1$ goods.) If point B is chosen, $0l_2$ hours will be spent in leisure, $l_m l_2$ hours in work, and $0x_2$ goods will be bought. But with the introduction of price search into the theory of consumer behavior, the consumer has a third alternative way to spend his time. To derive the budget constraint as modified by price search, first consider Figure 3.

Figure 3 shows the additional amounts of the commodity the consumer can purchase because of the discovery of lower prices. Quantity is measured on the vertical axis and search time on the horizontal. The y-intercept of each curve in Figure 3 shows the quantity of goods that the consumer can buy, given no additional price information. However, if the consumer spends time searching, it was shown in Figure 1 that he will find lower prices. Thus the positive slope of the curve $x = f_1(p)$ in Figure 3 reflects the fact that as more time is invested in searches for lower prices and these lower prices are found, the total quantity of x that the consumer is able to purchase increases.

---

[3] If the consumer were to find the lowest price, then further search would be useless and the consumer would be in the typical theoretical world of fixed prices. To assure that search is rewarding in each period, it is assumed that either the consumer "forgets" some of his prior information or the prices in the market change from period to period.

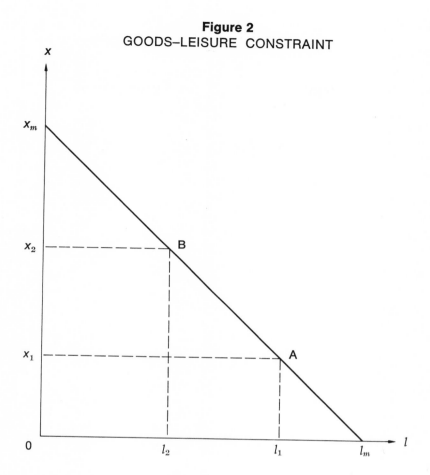

Figure 2
GOODS–LEISURE CONSTRAINT

Suppose, from Figure 2, that $0l_1$ leisure and $0x_1$ goods are chosen by the consumer who has no search alternative. In Figure 3 this choice is reflected in $0x_1$ goods and zero search. Now suppose the consumer can search and find lower prices. With the same amount of work, he can search, say, $0s_1$ hours and find prices low enough for him to be able to buy x_1x_3 more goods. (Of course, when he searches $0s_1$ hours he simultaneously reduces his leisure time by that exact amount.) With more searches (and less leisure) the consumer is able to buy even more goods because of even lower prices.

If the amounts of goods and leisure in Figure 2 were $0x_2$ instead of $0x_1$ and $0l_2$ instead of $0l_1$, the corresponding y-intercept in Figure 3 is x_2. With a greater quantity of the commodity now being purchased,

13

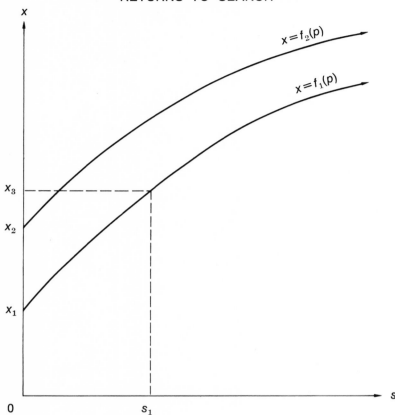

Figure 3
RETURNS TO SEARCH

the return to search increases. The new search function $x = f_2(p)$ is drawn higher than $x = f_1(p)$ to demonstrate the proportionately greater returns. Additional searches by the consumer will result in lower prices and greater quantities of x purchased.

A search curve for each possible quantity of x may be similarly derived and explained. After all such curves are drawn, the resulting field of curves shows the various options open to the consumer for increasing his real income (x) at all levels of goods and search.

To see the effects of search time on the conventional budget constraint, consider a point A on $x_m l_m$ in Figure 4. Traditional analysis (Figure 2) implies that at this particular work-leisure choice, $0l_1$ leisure and $0x_1$ goods can be consumed. The only way to consume more x is

14

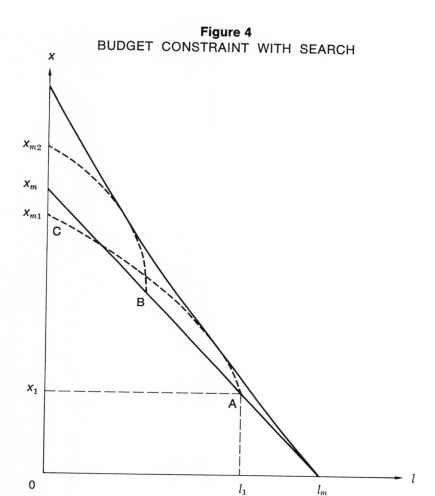

Figure 4
BUDGET CONSTRAINT WITH SEARCH

to work more and enjoy less leisure (and vice versa). In Figure 3 it was shown that with search added to the model, the consumer can, still with $l_m l_1$ work time, choose to enjoy less leisure and instead search for lower prices of x. With, say, $0x_1$ goods earned by $l_m l_1$ work, Figure 3 shows $x = f_1(p)$ to be the appropriate search function for the individual. Since with a given x the consumer's choice is between search and leisure, and work is the constant measure $l_m l_1$, curve $x = f_1(p)$ may be translated to Figure 4 such that zero search time coincides with l_1 on the work-leisure axis. Search time is thus measured from l_1 toward the $0x$ axis, while leisure is still measured

15

from the origin as before. The search function $x = f_1(p)$ so translated is $x_{m1}A$. It shows, with a given x_1, the additional amounts of x that can be purchased because of lower prices found with search. It also shows the remaining amount of leisure that can be enjoyed after each search alternative.

In like manner, each curve in the field of search curves in Figure 3 may be translated to Figure 4. For instance, curve $x = f_2(p)$ in Figure 3 translates to $x_{m2}B$ in Figure 4.

The curve described by the envelope of the linear budget constraint and the field of search functions in Figure 4 is the new budget constraint for the consumer. It is the locus of points that represents the maximum amount of goods attainable with optimum division of search effort and leisure for each of a series of work quantities.[4] Note that some portions of the translated search functions are above (to the right of) the linear budget constraint and some portions below. Those portions that are above the linear budget constraint reflect the assumption that the consumer is efficient enough in search to make it worthwhile to invest some time in search, since the return to search is greater than the wage rate.[5] Note also that the budget envelope is convex to the origin.[6] In order to assure a unique equilibrium it is necessary only to assume the consumer's utility curves are more convex than the budget constraint.

Just as a change in the wage rate affects the consumer's linear budget constraint, so does a change in search efficiency affect the budget envelope.[7] An increase in search efficiency, by rotating each of the search curves upward, would rotate the budget envelope upward about the maximum leisure point l_m. A decrease would rotate

---

[4] When the marginal return to search equals the marginal return to work, the consumer is allocating time optimally. This envelope in Figure 4 is the locus of points at which the marginal returns to search and work are equal. To distinguish it from the usual linear budget constraint, the search-modified constraint will be termed the "budget envelope."

[5] At the other extreme, it is quite possible that all portions of each search function lie below the linear budget constraint. In this case, the consumer is so inefficient in search that he is unable to find prices low enough to justify the search time invested. The net result is that the consumer would not search at all; he would face fixed prices and thus be in the conventional model without the search alternative.

[6] As the consumer earns more income and searches more, each successive reduction in price frees additional funds for more purchases. The returns to search, $-x \left(\frac{\partial p}{\partial s} \right)$, thus increase more than in proportion to income.

[7] The term "search efficiency" is used to refer to the price-reducing capability of the consumer: The more efficient is a consumer, the greater in absolute value is $\left(\frac{\partial p}{\partial s} \right)$.

the budget envelope downward, perhaps even below $l_m F$ (see Figure 5). In this case, it would lead the consumer to maximize utility by not searching at all. A change in the wage rate would operate on the budget envelope in a slightly different manner. An increase in the wage rate would rotate the budget line upward. Each search curve would be shifted horizontally to the right in accordance with the translation technique explained in the derivation of Figure 4. The final effect of an increase in the wage rate would be an upward rotation of the budget envelope. Changes in the wage rate would have different effects from changes in search efficiency because of the differences in rotation of the linear budget constraint versus rotation of the search curves. The general effect, a rotation of the budget envelope about l_m, would be the same for both.

Figure 5 depicts the determination of equilibrium levels of leisure, work, search, and goods. Given a utility maximizing tangency between budget constraint $x_m l_m$ and indifference curve II at point A, BC is the search function also tangent to II at A. At this choice of work time ($l_m E$), the maximum amount of goods possible without search is $0x_1$, but $0\hat{x}$ with search. The distance $0x_1$ is thus the amount of x consumed through expenditure of income earned in $l_m E$ hours of work. With price search of DE, $x_1\hat{x}$ more goods can be bought, leaving $0D$ hours of leisure. The optimal goods-time trade-off is thus found to be $0\hat{x}$ goods, $l_m E$ work time, DE search time, and $0D$ leisure. Without price search, $0\hat{x}$ goods could have been purchased only by giving up some of $0D$ leisure.[8]

Figure 5 clearly shows the return to the consumer from search and the allocation of alternative uses of time that achieves maximum utility for the consumer. It depicts the determination of allocation of time as the result of a simultaneous solution for search, work, leisure, and commodities.

Search Efficiency

Consumers who are more efficient at searching for low prices will be able to find better buys than those who are less efficient. Some consumers are better shoppers, are better able to budget their time carefully, and are better educated than others. However, the subject of this inquiry is not the personal determinants of search efficiency, but the origins of search efficiency in the marketplace. We are

---

[8] Note that this does not say that the search time does not have to be taken after all hours of work have been completed. Search can be undertaken during any nonwork hours in the planning period, for the consumer decides simultaneously the total number of hours to be spent in search, work, and leisure.

Figure 5
CONSUMER EQUILIBRIUM

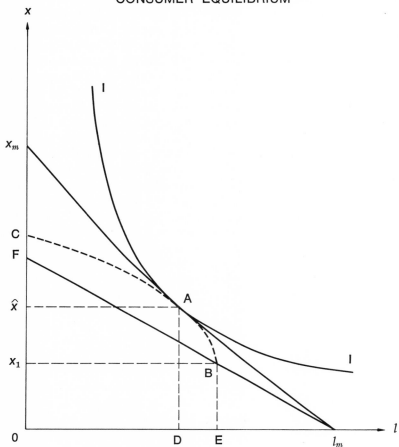

interested, for example, in the increase in the expected return to
search for low air conditioner prices that would be brought about by
a rash of fall air conditioner sales. In this example, as in the examination of gasoline sales that follows, all consumers gain in search
efficiency irrespective of differences in search efficiency traceable to
personal characteristics.

According to the theory presented in this study, consumers in
areas where gasoline stations post prices are more efficient at finding
lower prices than those elsewhere. Consumers who live where prices
are posted can determine the prices of one or more grades of gasoline

merely by driving past a station. Without price posting, the consumer has to pull into the station (perhaps after having to circle the block to get in the appropriate turn lane) and inspect each pump. Clearly, even the relatively inefficient searcher is made more efficient by price posting. Consumers who live where prices are posted can obtain more information per unit of search (or engage in less search per unit of information obtained) than other consumers.

Increases in search efficiency that originate in the marketplace create feedback effects on the structure of market prices. In the gasoline example, the high-price stations will observe a loss in patronage as more and more low-price stations post prices. The high-price stations will be forced to cut their prices or improve service in order to stave off further losses to the low-price stations. In the end, only the more efficient firms will be left operating and the average price of gasoline will fall. With the high-price firms out of the market and more consumers buying at the lower prices, the dispersion or spread of prices will be lower. Consumers will search less than they did before price posting began because the reduced price dispersion will have reduced the return to search. Searchers and nonsearchers alike will buy gasoline at lower prices and with less search. Finally, the market will be cleared of inefficient, high-price firms.

3
RETAIL GASOLINE

Retail price information, although costly to obtain, is important to the ability of a competitive economy to provide goods and services at the lowest possible social cost. When the flow of this information is impeded, the ability of consumers to identify the best buy is restricted and competition is reduced. It is expected that reduced competition will result in a higher level of prices and a lower level of consumer welfare.

Previous Studies

Previous investigation revealed that several major cities in the nation prohibit the posting of the retail price of gasoline on large signs visible to the passing motorist.[1] An examination of data released by the U.S. Bureau of Labor Statistics revealed that the dispersion of regular and premium prices in these cities was greater than in major cities that did not prohibit such price posting; a recent reanalysis of this data by Howard Marvel (who obtained more information about the size of the sample in each of the cities surveyed) reveals that a significant difference in dispersion exists only for premium and not for regular grade.[2] No firm conclusion was reached about

---

[1] Alex Maurizi, "The Effect of Laws against Price Advertising: The Case of Retail Gasoline," *Western Economic Journal*, vol. 10, no. 3 (September 1972), p. 323.

[2] Ibid., pp. 323-24. More recent investigation by Marvel reveals that this finding pertains only to premium and not to regular grade gasoline. Maurizi's investigation was based on information that "approximately" fifteen stations were sampled in each city. Marvel obtained more information about the nature of the sample, however; in several cities only twelve stations were sampled and in others eighteen were sampled. When he conducted Maurizi's analysis on groupings of equal sample size, his findings emerged. See Howard Marvel, "Gasoline Price Signs and Price Behavior: Comment," *Economic Inquiry*, forth-

the difference in the average level of prices in the two groups of cities.[3]

In the earlier of two recent studies of several aspects of the effects of consumer search in the retail gasoline market, Marvel found that stations with higher-priced gasoline are the most likely to have customers defect to other stations when consumers search more.[4] He also found that a decrease in search costs led to a decrease in price dispersion. However, this earlier study is not very useful for analyzing the effects of advertising on prices, since Marvel did not examine those factors that determine the level of prices. Instead, he examined those factors that determine price dispersion. (In his later study Marvel analyzes the level of retail prices and concludes that well-informed consumers help promote competition and eliminate market collusion.)

Marvel concluded in his earlier study that differences in gasoline price dispersion among cities are greater than the differences that could result from varying retailing techniques. This study argues that when a station decides to post prices it is choosing a retailing technique that itself explains some of the variation in gasoline prices.

Previous investigation was severely limited by the quality and availability of data collected by the Bureau of Labor Statistics. Only twelve to eighteen gasoline stations were sampled in each of the ten largest cities. Moreover, the confidentiality of data collected from individual stations and of mean price and sampling variance per-

coming. It is clear that the data used in Maurizi's previous study are far from ideal for purposes of policy analysis; the sample size is very small and there is inadequate information about the stations sampled. In comparison, the data used in the current investigation are far better suited for policy analysis. Happily, the findings are as expected regarding both the average price and the dispersion of prices in this study. Marvel's suggestion that price posting is less common for premium than regular grades is supported by our data, but his suggestion that this explains the significant findings for premium in his re-analysis of the earlier data is not supported by the findings of the current investigation. See Maurizi, "Gasoline Price Signs and Price Behavior: A Reply," *Economic Inquiry*, forthcoming.

[3] Maurizi, "Effect of Laws against Price Advertising," pp. 323-28. Allen suggests this result should have been expected. He argues that price advertising can help promote and maintain cartels by making it easier to administer them. As a result, average prices might be increased by price advertising. See Bruce Allen, "Advertising and Gasoline Prices: Comment," *Economic Inquiry*, vol. 14, no. 3 (September 1976), pp. 457-58. The evidence presented in this study indicates Allen's conjecture is incorrect, since prices are found to be lower where there is greater posting intensity.

[4] See Howard P. Marvel, "The Economics of Information and Retail Gasoline Price Behavior: An Empirical Analysis," *Journal of Political Economy*, vol. 84, no. 5 (October 1976), pp. 1033-60 for the earlier study and Howard P. Marvel, "Competition and Price Levels in the Retail Gasoline Market," *Review of Economics and Statistics*, forthcoming, for the later study.

mitted only the range of prices to be reported.[5] Thus, one could not control for individual station characteristics that affect gasoline prices, such as whether the station offered trading stamps, was a major or independent brand retailer, or offered self-service. Furthermore, the data did not contain any information regarding the proportion of stations posting their prices in each of the cities. The analysis of policy options regarding price posting laws need not be limited by data of such low quality, however. Fortunately, better data are available.

Lundberg Survey Data

The Lundberg survey is conducted by a firm that collects information on the retail gasoline industry in the United States. This information is provided to interested parties including major and nonmajor refiners and suppliers (sometimes referred to as "wholesalers"), private brand operators, and government agency users.[6] Information is collected on the station's location, whether the station is a major or independent, the date of the survey, the pump price for each grade of gasoline sold, and whether the price is a self-service or an attended price. One piece of information important for our purposes is whether each pump price was also posted at the station's premises on a large sign visible to passing motorists. In view of their importance here, it is worth noting that the Lundberg data are generally regarded as being highly reliable.

The Study Period and Sample Selected. For purposes of analysis it is important to select a period before the imposition of U.S. wage and price controls in August 1971. The prices compared must be those generated by a market in which price is not controlled directly by a federal or state agency. The study period was also limited by the fact that the Lundberg data are readily available for the desired areas only since November 1970. Finally, the availability of other relevant data needed in the analysis was an important consideration. In particular, the availability of income data from the 1970 Census dictated a period as close as possible to the year of the census, that is, 1969. Thus the month of November 1970 was chosen as the study period, and one day (Julian date 326 in 1970) during this month (on which Lundberg

---

[5] Maurizi, "Effect of Laws against Price Advertising," p. 323, fn. 7.

[6] The Lundberg survey publications are self-described as gasoline industry publications. See, for example, *Lundberg Letter*. Other industry publications frequently refer to the results of the Lundberg survey as a source of reliable data. See, for example, "Long 'Spreads,' Frantic Pricing Stirs New Problems," *National Petroleum News* (May 1975), pp. 50-57.

conducted its monthly or biweekly survey) was chosen for analysis. Appendix B contains a description of the sample in each of six California areas, seven other western urban areas, and four geographical areas comprising the metropolitan New York City region.

This study analyzes the effects of posting on the price of two types of gasoline: leaded regular and leaded premium gasoline. These two types of gasoline were selected to ensure a large enough sample for analysis. Since the data account only for attended prices in 1970, they are associated with "full-service" (the attendant fills the tank, cleans the windshield, and checks the oil and battery). This omission should not significantly affect the results, since, despite the development of self-service features at major-brand stations, over 93 percent of all major-brand-name stations still provided full-service as late as January 1975.

The recent trend to other forms of service is evident from the fact that only 73 percent of all major stations provided only full-service by January 1976. The most common development is that of the split-island station, with full-service at one island of a station and self-service at another island. While split-island stations accounted for only 5 percent of all stations in January 1975, they accounted for 24 percent in January 1976. Complete self-service major-brand stations accounted for only 2 percent in 1975 but almost 4 percent in 1976.[7] By July 1977 split-island and complete self-service stations accounted for one-third of all gasoline being pumped at service stations. The trend to self-service was spurred along, industry experts indicate, by the high price of gasoline resulting from the Arab oil embargo.[8] In 1975 and 1976, self-service prices at major-brand stations averaged approximately 2 cents to 2.5 cents per gallon lower than full-service prices for each grade of gasoline for all stations in the United States.[9] Clearly, any study of very recent price data would need to examine self-service station prices also.[10]

---

[7] Lundberg survey, *Lundberg Letter*, vol. 3, no. 11 (January 16, 1976), p. 3.

[8] See "One of Every Three Gallons Is Pumped by Customer," *Sacramento Bee*, August 12, 1977, which reports the latest American Petroleum Institute figures.

[9] Lundberg survey, *Comprehensive Price Report*, January 9, 1976, parts 1 (Full-service) and 2 (Self-service).

[10] Among the states in which the cities analyzed in this study are located, self-service retail gasoline marketing was prohibited by Oregon, permitted only with an attendant by both Arizona and Utah, and permitted at the option of the locality in California, Colorado, Idaho, Nevada, New York, and Washington in 1971. "Where Self-service Marketing Is Legal," *National Petroleum News: Factbook Issue*, vol. 64 (mid-May 1972), p. 114.

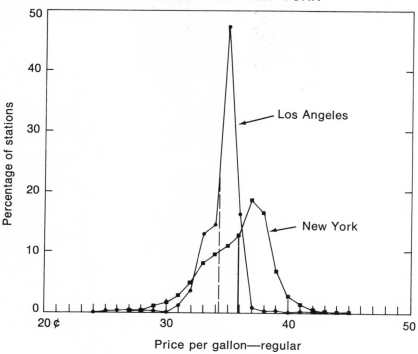

Figure 6
DISTRIBUTION OF PRICES OF REGULAR GASOLINE IN
LOS ANGELES AND NEW YORK

A New Approach: Los Angeles v. New York. The simplest way to illustrate the results of this investigation is to compare the distribution of prices in two cities of similar size that have opposite price-posting rules. Because the city of New York prohibited price posting in 1970, less than 10 percent of all the stations in the metropolitan area of New York City (which includes the city but extends beyond the city boundaries into the Long Island, White Plains, and New Jersey areas) posted their prices. In contrast, because the city of Los Angeles permitted price posting, over 90 percent of all stations in the Los Angeles metropolitan area posted regular prices and over 70 percent posted premium prices in 1970.[11]

Figure 6 provides the frequency distribution of prices for leaded regular for these two areas. The mean of the distribution for Los

---

[11] In California, the cities of Los Angeles, Oakland, and San Francisco now require the posting of retail gasoline prices.

Figure 7

DISTRIBUTION OF PRICES OF PREMIUM GASOLINE IN LOS ANGELES AND NEW YORK

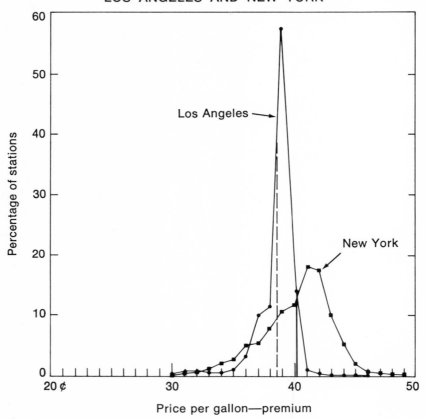

Price per gallon—premium

Angeles (indicated by the dashed vertical line) is 1½ cents lower than that for New York (indicated by the solid vertical line). Moreover, the spread of prices is dramatically different in Los Angeles. Approximately 64 percent of the Los Angeles prices are located within 1 cent of the modal price, whereas only 33 percent of the New York prices are located within 1 cent of the modal price. The distribution of regular grade prices is much more sharply peaked and much less widely dispersed in Los Angeles than in New York. Figure 7 is a graph of the distribution of premium prices in Los Angeles and New York. A similar situation prevails. Over 72 percent of Los Angeles prices are within 1 cent of the modal price, whereas only

35 percent of New York prices are within 1 cent of the modal price. The distribution of Los Angeles premium prices is even more sharply peaked than the distribution of Los Angeles regular prices, whereas the distribution of New York premium prices is similar to the distribution of New York regular prices. The difference between the distributions of Los Angeles and New York prices is statistically significant for both regular and premium grades.[12] (Appendix Tables B-2 and B-3 provide the data on which Figures 6 and 7 are based.)

Since market prices are commonly assumed to be normally distributed,[13] it is interesting to note that, for both premium and regular grades, neither Los Angeles nor New York regular prices are normally distributed. The differences between the observed distributions and the normal distribution are statistically significant.[14]

Finally, even if the price distributions in both cities are standardized by subtracting each price from the mean price and dividing by the sample standard deviation, the two distributions remain significantly different.[15] Figure 8 displays the standardized distributions for regular and Figure 9 displays them for premium prices. In other words, it is not possible to obtain the distribution of prices in Los Angeles from that in New York by a suitable alteration in the mean and dispersion of prices. The Los Angeles distribution remains more highly peaked and less widely dispersed than the New York distribution. (See Appendix Tables B-4 and B-5.)

---

[12] The Kolmogorov-Smirnov statistical test of the difference between two cumulative distribution functions was used for this purpose. This test essentially is based upon the maximum of the differences in height between the two cumulative distributions. The larger the maximum difference, the more likely the two cumulative distributions are not the same. The test statistic in the case of the distribution of Los Angeles v. New York leaded regular prices amounts to .46 and in the case of the distribution of Los Angeles v. New York leaded premium prices amounts to .53. The critical 1 percent level value in the former case equals .041 and in the latter case equals .038, so the null hypothesis of equality between the two cumulative distributions must be rejected. See Sidney Siegel, *Nonparametric Statistics* (New York: McGraw-Hill, 1956), pp. 127-37.

[13] See, for example, George Stigler, "The Economics of Information," *Journal of Political Economy*, vol. 60 (June 1961), p. 215.

[14] The Kolmogorov-Smirnov test statistic for the difference between the cumulative distribution of leaded regular prices and the hypothesized cumulative normal distribution of leaded regular prices equals .18 in Los Angeles; for leaded premium v. the hypothesized cumulative normal distribution it equals .07. Both statistics are significant at the 1 percent level, so the hypothesis that the cumulative distribution of prices is the same as a normal distribution with the same mean and variance must be rejected. In New York, the test statistics equal .21 and .08; both are significant at the 1 percent level.

[15] The Kolmogorov-Smirnov test statistic for the difference between the cumulative standardized distributions of leaded regular prices equals .12 and of leaded premium prices equals .20, both significant at the 1 percent level.

Figure 8

STANDARDIZED DISTRIBUTION OF PRICES OF REGULAR GASOLINE IN LOS ANGELES AND NEW YORK

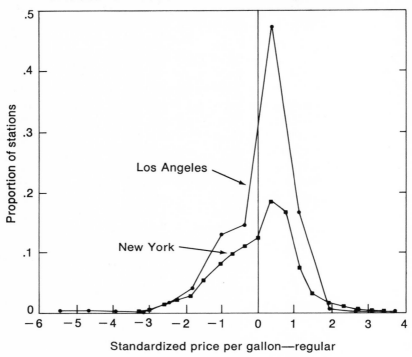

Standardized price per gallon—regular

Expanding the Sample. New York and Los Angeles are of special interest because they are the two largest cities at opposite ends of the price-posting spectrum. The above comparisons were made to illustrate the differences in distributions and suggest one explanation for these differences.

The next test of the impact of posting intensity on prices and their dispersion is conducted on an expanded sample of data from all fourteen geographical areas (counting the four New York areas as one). The purpose in conducting this test is to identify those factors that might be responsible for the differences in prices among cities, to measure the relative impacts of the factors, and to determine the extent to which the observed price differences are ascribable to differences in the proportion of stations posting prices.

Figure 9

STANDARDIZED DISTRIBUTION OF PRICES OF PREMIUM GASOLINE IN LOS ANGELES AND NEW YORK

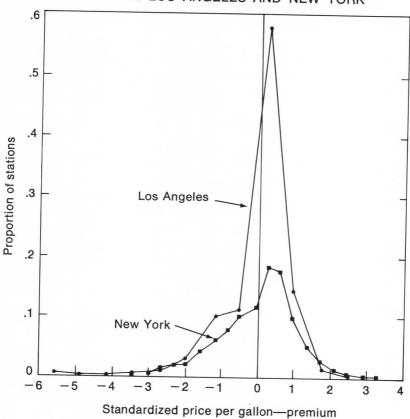

Standardized price per gallon—premium

Variables

As before, the focus is on differences in retail gasoline prices. It is hypothesized that, other things being equal, more intense price posting in an area will be associated with lower prices.[16] The following

---

[16] For a more extensive discussion of the theory of search and how it relates to advertising of price, the reader is referred to Stigler, "Economics of Information," pp. 213-25; Stigler, "Information in the Labor Market," *Journal of Political Economy*, supplement vol. 70 (October 1962), pp. 94-105; Stigler, *The Organization of Industry* (Homewood, Ill.: Irwin, 1968), chapter 16; Lester Telser, "Advertising and Competition," *Journal of Political Economy*, vol. 72 (December 1974), pp. 537-62.

is a discussion of each variable, including the intensity of price posting, that is expected to affect prices.

Posting and Posting Intensity. Two impacts of price posting are examined: the impact of an individual station's decision to post, and the impact of the posting intensity in the entire area. The station posting its prices is expected to post them because it has a competitive advantage over other similar stations in the area and wants potential customers to know that it can offer the same product at a lower price. The posting of prices lowers search costs for some potential customers and increases the chance of a sale to a new customer. The extent to which search costs are lowered, however, depends upon the number of other stations in the area that also post prices. If only one station in an entire area posts its prices, for example, potential customers must still drive into other stations to inspect the pump price for comparison. However, if all other stations post prices, then motorists can observe all prices merely by driving past each station. Since comparison shopping is costly, a station's posted price need not be much lower than the unposted prices of several of the station's nearest competitors. However, with comparison shopping made cheaper by increased posting intensity, the posted price will be even lower than the unposted price owing to the much broader nature of the competition.

Two variables are introduced to account for this distinction—first, a variable to indicate whether a given station posts its prices (stations posting prices are expected to have lower prices than those not posting prices, other factors being held constant) and second, a variable for the proportion of all stations in the metropolitan area that post their prices (the greater this proportion, the more efficiently can consumers search and so the lower prices in the area are expected to be). To distinguish between these variables, the first will be referred to as the "posting" variable while the second will be referred to as the "posting intensity" variable. Since this investigation is designed to determine the extent to which Los Angeles prices, say, are lower because so great a proportion of stations post their prices, the principal focus is on the posting intensity variable and its impact on price levels. In particular, for each area, the proportion of all stations selling leaded regular gasoline that posted the price of leaded regular gasoline is defined as the intensity of price posting for leaded regular gasoline. Similarly, in each area the proportion of all stations selling leaded premium gasoline that posted the price of leaded premium is defined as the intensity of price posting for leaded premium gasoline.

Brand. One factor that affects price is the brand of gasoline being sold. Traditionally, the price of gasoline sold by major oil companies is several cents higher than that sold by independent oil companies.[17] A "major" oil company is generally defined to be one of the large, integrated firms that combines crude oil exploration and production with refining, distribution, and retail sales.[18] Independents typically do not explore for and produce crude oil but instead rely on other sources of crude oil.[19] Gasoline is also being sold at retail by other outlets with no refinery capacity, such as major discount department stores or neighborhood convenience stores.[20] Since 1972, when majors constituted over 77 percent of all retail sales and private-brand independents constituted only 8 percent of sales, the share of majors has fallen to under 74 percent and the share of independents has risen to over 11 percent.[21]

Since a significant price differential is expected to exist between majors and independents, a variable indicating whether a station was a major or independent dealer is introduced to account for this effect.

Income. Although changes in the level of income will exert an effect on the amount of price search, the direction of that effect cannot be determined a priori. On the one hand, people with low incomes (typically the result of low hourly earnings) will have an incentive to conduct more search activity since the opportunity cost of their time is low. On the other hand, people with high incomes will also be

---

[17] "Price spreads, traditionally a serious competitive factor at the 2¢-gal. level, have mushroomed in many markets to an unbelievable average of 4¢ to 6¢ gal., with extremes shooting wildly upwards to highs of 11¢ gal.", "Long 'Spreads'," p. 50. See also Robert Masson and Fred Allvine, "Strategies and Structures: Majors, Independents and Prices of Gasoline in Local Markets," in Robert Masson and David Qualls, eds., *Essays on Industrial Organization in Honor of Joe S. Bain* (Cambridge, Mass.: Ballinger, 1976), pp. 155-80, particularly.

[18] A list of the integrated firms typically surveyed by the Lundberg survey for trends in market share are: Amoco, Arco, Citgo, Conoco, Exxon, Gulf, Mobil, Phillips, Shell, Skelly, Socal, Sohio, Sunoco, Texaco, Union. See Lundberg survey, *Lundberg Letter*, vol. 2, no. 43 (August 29, 1975), p. 5. The same letter also presents monthly price spreads (retail and wholesale) between the majors and independents for 1975 on p. 6. The above integrated firms constituted approximately two-thirds of the national gasoline market in 1975. See *National Petroleum News: Factbook Issue*, vol. 68, no. 5A (mid-May 1976), p. 89.

[19] For a recent discussion of the structure of the industry at the discovery, production, and refining levels see M. A. Adelman, *The World Petroleum Market* (Baltimore: Johns Hopkins Press, 1972), pp. 78-100.

[20] "Convenience Stores: More Sell Gasoline," *National Petroleum News: Factbook Issue*, vol. 64 (mid-May 1972), p. 58. In 1971 there were over 21,000 convenience-type food stores selling gasoline, comprising 15 percent of all such stores.

[21] "Long 'Spreads'," p. 56.

more likely to purchase more items (such as gallons of gasoline) or items that are more expensive (such as premium rather than regular grade gasoline) for which the gains from additional search will be high. Thus, it is an empirical question whether additional price search is conducted more by low-income or high-income people.

The *1970 Census of Population* provides average family income levels for each of the major standard metropolitan statistical areas in the country for the year 1969.[22] A variable was constructed consisting of this family income level for each metropolitan area in the sample analyzed.

Gasoline Taxes. Among the metropolitan areas studied there were some differences in the level of statewide gasoline taxes. Arizona, California, Idaho, New York, New Jersey, and Oregon all collected 7 cents per gallon while Nevada collected 6 cents and Washington 9 cents. A variable is introduced to control for the differences in prices that would be due to state gasoline tax differences. (The federal 4-cents-per-gallon tax on gasoline applies equally to all states in the country.) This variable does not include statewide gasoline sales taxes, county gasoline taxes, municipal gasoline taxes, or other local gasoline taxes. Although New York State appears to be the only one in our study to have levied a sales tax on gasoline in 1970, available sources do not indicate which municipalities or counties did levy a gasoline tax. The one state in our sample which prohibited local gasoline taxes (Washington) is known, and one state having both county and municipal taxes (Nevada) is known, but in other states (California, New Jersey, New York, Oregon) there is no legal provision respecting local gasoline taxes.[23] In these cases it is difficult to determine whether any such taxes are levied. Accordingly, in order to determine whether the results are seriously affected by the way we have measured taxes on gasoline, a separate analysis is also conducted for all California stations. We have been able to determine that there were no statewide sales taxes, county taxes, or municipal taxes levied on gasoline in California in 1970. From the time California state and local sales and use taxes were instituted, gasoline was specifically exempt, since its distribution was already subject to a Motor Vehicle

---

22 U.S. Bureau of the Census, *1970 Census of Population* (Washington, D.C., 1970).

23 "State Gasoline Tax Table," U.S. Internal Revenue Service, *Instructions for Schedule A (Form 1040)*, 1970, p. 8; "State Gasoline Tax Rates 1919-1970," American Petroleum Institute, *Petroleum Facts and Figures: 1971*, Washington, D.C., p. 473; and American Petroleum Institute Committee on Public Affairs, *Tax Compendium*, New York, 1970, especially Tables TC-9, TC-11 and TC-33.

Fuel License Tax. (This exemption for gasoline was deleted by the Transportation Development Act of 1971, chapter 1400, effective July 1, 1972.) [24] Moreover, California contains six of the fourteen areas studied (considering the four New York areas as one) and therefore represents an area where the posting intensity variable would vary in value enough to allow reliable estimation to be conducted. This separate analysis will indicate that our results are not seriously affected by the way we have measured taxes on gasoline.

Wholesale Prices. The higher the level of wholesale prices in an area, the higher the expected level of retail prices. Unfortunately, the available wholesale price data are for regular grade only and do not account for all the cities analyzed in this study.[25] Moreover, there are some deficiencies associated with the available wholesale price data. Observed wholesale prices differ significantly from actual wholesale prices owing to the suppliers' practice of offering "allowances" and "discounts" to dealers. Although data on observed wholesale prices are generally available, data on wholesale prices adjusted for allowances and discounts are not.[26]

The principal purpose of dealer discounts is to allow suppliers to practice what amounts to price discrimination. The practice of giving such discounts enables suppliers to restrict wholesale price reductions to dealers affected by price wars (which are typically triggered by the growth and entry of independent dealers in an area). A relatively high wholesale price is quoted to all dealers in the same metropolitan area, but sizable discounts and allowances are made locally where needed to help individual dealers survive a war.[27] The less likely it is that a price war will remain localized, the more likely it is that a supplier will choose to quote a lower wholesale price to all dealers and to allow relatively small individual discounts, if any.

Price wars are more likely to be localized if there is little or no price posting. Thus, observed wholesale prices tend to be biased upward in those areas where there is little or no posting of prices

[24] *West's Annotated California Codes*, 1971, Revenue and Taxation Code, Div. 2, parts 1.5, 2.

[25] "Gas Prices in 55 Cities: 1971," *National Petroleum News: Factbook Issue*, vol. 64 (mid-May 1972), p. 107. The source of the data reported is *Platt's Oilgram Service*.

[26] Maurizi, "Effect of Laws against Price Advertising," pp. 323, 325-28. See also Masson and Allvine, "Strategies and Structures," p. 165.

[27] See Masson and Allvine, "Strategies and Structures," pp. 162-65 and 173 for discussion of the notion that actual wholesale prices to majors are lower in areas near independent stations. They find that price wars are a strategy used by the majors to reduce the growth of competition by independents (pp. 169-79).

and, hence, where retail prices are expected to be higher. The expected positive relation between wholesale and retail prices should be strengthened by this bias (if the relation is significant it could be due to this bias).

Trading Stamps. Finally, the effect of a station's decision to provide trading stamps to customers is expected to influence the price it charges. A station's prices are expected to be higher if it issues trading stamps, other factors being held constant.[28] A variable has been constructed to indicate the presence or absence of trading stamps in order to adjust for this effect.

Results

The results, shown in Table 1, report leaded regular prices separately from leaded premium prices. The results support the expectations regarding the signs of the regression coefficients. The posting variable, which is zero for stations not posting and unity for stations posting, is negatively related to price. The simple act of price posting is associated with a retail price reduction of about 1 cent per gallon for leaded regular and of about 0.8 cent per gallon for leaded premium. More importantly, the intensity of price posting is also negatively related to the retail price. The impact differs substantially between the two grades of gasoline. A 50 percent increase in the proportion of stations in an area posting the price of leaded regular, say, from .61 to .92, would result in a regular price decline of about 0.3 cent per gallon ($.31 \times .94 \approx .30$). A 50 percent increase in the proportion of stations in an area posting the price of leaded premium, say, from .53 to .79, however, would result in a premium price decline of approximately 0.6 cent per gallon ($.26 \times 2.30 \approx .60$).

Perhaps the effect can be illustrated more dramatically by comparing again the New York and Los Angeles areas. In the New York metropolitan area, only 12 percent of all stations selling leaded regular and 9 percent of all stations selling leaded premium posted these respective prices. (Although in the city of New York the posting of prices by retail gasoline stations was illegal during the study period, our sample of stations from the metropolitan area includes stations outside the city limits; only 1 percent of the stations in the Great Neck, Hempstead, Queens, Valley Stream, Brooklyn, and Manhattan areas—the sections of the metropolitan area most com-

---

[28] Ibid, p. 166.

Table 1
REGRESSION RESULTS: U.S. RETAIL GASOLINE PRICES, NOVEMBER 1970

Variable	Leaded Regular			Leaded Premium		
	Mean value	Coefficient	t-value	Mean value	Coefficient	t-value
Retail price	36.10			40.20		
Posting[a]	.61	−1.02	22.89	.53	−.79	26.61
Posting intensity	.61	−.94	11.53	.54	−2.30	34.53
Major or independent[b]	.07	−2.81	41.31	.06	−3.77	68.06
Income[c]	10,748.00	.00011	6.13	10,786.00	.00014	10.09
Gas tax[d]	7.20	.71	25.44	7.20	.66	31.79
Stamps[e]	.43	.29	6.81	.49	.27	8.47
Constant		31.17			35.58	
R^2	.23			.35		
F	641.00			1,359.00		
DF	12,584.00			15,092.00		

[a] Dummy variable = 1 if price is posted by station, 0 if price is not posted by station.
[b] Dummy variable = 1 if independent-brand station, 0 if major-brand station.
[c] Mean value in dollars.
[d] Mean value in cents per gallon.
[e] Dummy variable = 1 if trading stamps issued by station, 0 if trading stamps not issued by station.

pletely within the city limits—posted either regular or premium prices.)

In contrast, in Los Angeles over 90 percent of all stations selling leaded regular posted regular prices and over 74 percent of all stations selling leaded premium posted premium prices. The regression results indicate that this difference in posting intensity would be responsible for leaded regular prices being 0.7 cent per gallon lower and leaded premium prices being 1.5 cents per gallon lower in Los Angeles than in New York City, other factors being held constant.

Prices at independent stations amounted to 2.81 cents per gallon less for leaded regular and 3.77 cents per gallon less for leaded premium. Independent retailers comprised 7 percent of all stations selling leaded regular and only 6 percent of all stations selling leaded premium. Thus, although there is a large price difference between the majors and the independents, the consumer benefit derived from this price difference is limited by the relatively small number of independent stations.

The effect of income alters average retail prices by only 0.11 cent per gallon for regular and 0.14 cent per gallon for premium for every $1,000 change in average family income. Thus, in areas where incomes are lower, the net effect is to cause increased search activity and, hence, somewhat lower prices. Higher-income families evidently do not find the benefits from increased search activity for low-priced gasoline to be worth the search cost.[29]

Issuing trading stamps increases leaded regular prices by 0.43 cent per gallon and leaded premium prices by 0.49 cent per gallon. The effect of higher gas taxes increases retail prices. As indicated in Table 2, for leaded regular the inclusion of the wholesale price variable does not alter these results. The wholesale price coefficient is positive, as expected, but not significant.

As indicated in Table 3, neither the signs of the coefficients nor their significance levels are altered when the analysis is conducted only for California stations so the gasoline tax variable can be removed. The California analysis was conducted, it will be recalled, to determine if any bias was present in the results because of the way we measured gasoline taxes. The value of the posting coefficient changed only slightly for both regular and premium. The value of the posting intensity coefficient became greater (in absolute value) for regular and smaller (in absolute value) for premium. These changes are offsetting; the total consumer benefits we calculate later would be slightly greater if the California posting intensity coefficients were to apply (owing to the greater percentage of total sales attributed to regular). Thus, for the purposes of our study there does not appear to be any serious bias introduced into the analysis as a result of the way we have measured taxes on gasoline (measuring only state gasoline taxes and excluding sales taxes, county taxes, and municipal taxes).

The statistical results are highly significant. The proportion of explained variation in retail prices, 23 percent for leaded regular and 35 percent for leaded premium, is surprisingly high for sample sizes of this magnitude (approximately 12,600 and 15,100 stations respectively).

---

[29] This income effect is a result of the complete income-work-leisure trade-off and therefore differs from the "windfall" income effect that is discussed in Appendix A.

Table 2

REGRESSION RESULTS: U.S. RETAIL GASOLINE PRICES, NOVEMBER 1970, WHOLESALE PRICE VARIABLE INCLUDED

Variable	Mean value	Leaded Regular Coefficient	t-value
Retail price		36.20	
Posting[a]	.60	− 1.05	21.30
Posting intensity	.60	− .91	10.20
Major or independent[b]	.08	− 2.70	37.08
Income[c]	10,870.00	.00017	8.22
Gas tax[d]	7.20	.73	20.52
Stamps[e]	.40	.26	5.36
Wholesale price[d]	18.43	.029	1.02
Constant .		29.80	
R^2	.23		
F	475.00		
DF	11,233.00		

[a] Dummy variable = 1 if price is posted by station, 0 if price is not posted by station.
[b] Dummy variable = 1 if independent-brand station, 0 if major-brand station.
[c] Mean value in dollars.
[d] Mean value in cents per gallon.
[e] Dummy variable = 1 if trading stamps issued by station, 0 if trading stamps not issued by station.

Information Value in a Brand Name. Advertising by major-brand manufacturers may create product identifiability, which would make it easier for motorists to comparison shop among major-brand stations than among independent-brand stations. If this were the case, then the availability of retail price information through posting would be expected to have a greater impact on price levels among majors than among independents.

The appropriate test for any such difference would be conducted on major-brand stations and on independent-brand stations and would indicate whether any differences in the posting intensity coefficients were significant. Unfortunately, the sample does not contain sufficient data for both majors and independents among the cities selected to conduct this test. Instead, the group of majors was

Table 3

REGRESSION RESULTS: CALIFORNIA RETAIL GASOLINE PRICES, NOVEMBER 1970

Variable	Leaded Regular			Leaded Premium		
	Mean value	Coeffi-cient	*t*-value	Mean value	Coeffi-cient	*t*-value
Retail price	35.70			39.70		
Posting [a]	.81	−1.10	21.97	.69	−.77	24.77
Posting intensity	.81	−1.87	11.15	.69	−1.46	13.50
Major or inde-pendent [b]	.002	−3.63	8.96	.002	−3.93	10.90
Income [c]	10,931.11	−.00014	4.31	10,948.61	−.00009	4.05
Stamps [d]	.74	.41	9.60	.74	.39	12.19
Constant		39.27			42.00	
R^2		.16			.14	
F		206.61			265.72	
DF		5,620.00			8,208.00	

[a] Dummy variable = 1 if price is posted by station, 0 if price is not posted by station.
[b] Dummy variable = 1 if independent-brand station, 0 if major-brand station.
[c] Mean value in dollars.
[d] Dummy variable = 1 if trading stamps issued by station, 0 if trading stamps not issued by station.

analyzed to determine whether the posting intensity coefficient was different. Although the significance of any such difference cannot be determined, the direction of any such difference could be informative and could suggest further research.

Accordingly, Table 4 presents the analysis for majors only. The results indicate that the impact of the posting intensity variable is greater among majors than among majors and independents combined. The implication is that the price-reducing effects of price advertising directed at products advertised by manufacturers exceed the price-reducing effects of price advertising directed at products not advertised by manufacturers. This finding is consistent with the proposition that manufacturers' advertising gives a product identifiability, makes consumer search easier, and, hence, reduces consumer prices.

Table 4

REGRESSION RESULTS: U.S. RETAIL GASOLINE PRICES, NOVEMBER 1970, MAJORS ONLY

Variable	Leaded Regular			Leaded Premium		
	Mean value	Coefficient	t-value	Mean value	Coefficient	t-value
Retail price [a]	36.40			40.40		
Posting [b]	.60	−1.03	22.82	.55	−.77	25.66
Posting intensity	.60	−1.35	16.18	.55	−2.44	37.21
Income [c]	10,779.00	.00014	7.70	10,813.00	.000133	9.20
Gas tax [a]	7.20	.69	23.52	7.20	.65	29.77
Stamps [d]	.46	.39	8.97	.52	.25	8.21
Constant		31.12			35.89	
R^2		.15			.25	
F		415.00			923.00	
DF		11,664.00			14,177.00	

[a] Mean value in cents per gallon.

[b] Dummy variable = 1 if price is posted by station, 0 if price is not posted by station.

[c] Mean value in dollars.

[d] Dummy variable = 1 if trading stamps issued by station, 0 of trading stamps not issued by station.

Benefits of Competitive and Universal Posting

Since only 53 percent of all stations selling leaded premium and only 61 percent of all stations selling leaded regular posted their prices, it can be asked what would be the gains to consumers if more stations posted their prices for both these grades of gasoline. Consider first the result if the posting intensity in New York were as high as in Los Angeles, next the result if the posting intensity in all areas were as high as in Los Angeles, and finally the result if posting were universal in all areas.

Competitive Posting. In 1970 there were 89.9 billion gallons of gasoline sold in the nation.[30] The proportion consisting of premium gasoline varied across metropolitan areas, ranging in 1971 from 31.9

---

[30] "Here Are National, State Market Shares," *National Petroleum News: Factbook Issue*, vol. 64 (mid-May 1972), p. 116.

percent in Milwaukee to 69.3 percent in the Los Angeles–Long Beach area.[31] The estimated proportion consisting of premium was 50.3 percent in fifty-two major metropolitan areas in 1971 and 43 percent of all gasoline sales in 1970 in the United States as a whole.[32] We shall assume that 43 percent of all the gasoline sold in the nation in 1970 was leaded premium and that 57 percent was leaded regular.

In 1969, the most recent year for which data are available, total gasoline sales in the New York metropolitan area amounted to $851.9 million.[33] Premium accounted for 56 percent of all gasoline sales in New York in 1971.[34] Assuming these are accurate estimates of 1970 sales and the proportion of sales accounted for by premium sales, there were 1.187 billion gallons of premium sold and 1.047 billion gallons of regular sold in the New York area in 1970 (the average leaded regular price and leaded premium price were 35.8 cents and 40.2 cents, respectively, based on this study's sample data). If the proportion posting regular were to increase from .12 to .90 (the proportion for Los Angeles), an increase of .78, and the proportion posting premium were to increase from .09 to .74 (the proportion for Los Angeles), an increase of .65, then the average price of regular would be estimated on the basis of the results in Table 1 to fall by .73 cent per gallon (.78 × .94 = .73) and that for premium by 1.50 cents per gallon (.65 × 2.30 = 1.50). The social gain would have amounted to $7.6 million (.73¢ × 1.047 billion gallons = $7.6 million) from regular plus $17.8 million (1.50¢ × 1.187 billion = $17.8 million) from premium for a total of $25.4 million.

What would happen if the entire U.S. market were to become as competitive as the Los Angeles area retail gasoline market, where approximately 90 percent of the stations posted their regular grade prices and approximately 74 percent posted their premium grade prices in 1970? The gains in 1970 would have amounted to $138 million for regular and $186 million for premium for a total of $324 million. Using gallonage figures for 1975 instead of for 1970, however, changes these gains to $226 million for regular and to $96 million for premium for a total of $322 million.

Since 1970, however, average price levels have also risen considerably. The dollar impact of price posting can be expected to vary with the level of prices. High and rising prices would be expected to stimulate more search activity. Suppose that the value of the posting

---

[31] "Gasoline Sales by Grade," ibid., p. 80.
[32] National Petroleum News: Factbook Issue, vol. 64 (mid-May 1972), pp. 32, 80.
[33] American Petroleum Institute, Petroleum Facts and Figures, 1971.
[34] "Gasoline Sales by Grade," ibid., p. 80.

intensity coefficient were a fixed percentage of the average price. Since the average regular price at full-service stations in 1975 was 57.2 cents per gallon and average premium price was 61.8 cents per gallon, the values of the intensity of price posting coefficients under this assumption would be —1.48 and —3.52 for leaded regular and leaded premium, respectively.[35] The implication of these updated estimates for 1975 gallonage sold in the United States (1975 data are the most recent available) is that the posting intensity as great as in the Los Angeles area would have saved consumers $360 million for regular grade and $147 million for premium grade in 1975, or altogether $507 million. Of course, consumers would have chosen to use some of these savings to purchase more gasoline because of its lower price. The word "savings" here is intended to indicate the total increase in consumer purchasing power (welfare) brought about by increased posting intensity.

Universal Posting. If the proportion of all stations posting leaded regular prices had increased from 61 percent to 100 percent, the regression results tell us, as shown in Table 5, that the average price of leaded regular would have been reduced by approximately .4 cent for each of the 51.2 billion gallons sold (or by approximately $189 million). Similarly, if the proportion of all stations posting leaded premium prices had increased from 53 percent to 100 percent, the average price of leaded premium would have been reduced by approximately 1.1 cents per gallon for each of the 38.7 billion gallons sold due to the greater intensity of posting (or approximately $418 million). This amounts to a grand total of $607 million annually for 1970. Given that 1975 consumption rose to 103.6 billion gallons but that premium sales fell to 19.2 percent,[36] the total cost saving fell from $607 million to $525 million (assuming, as shown in Table 6, the same posting intensity and the same effects of posting intensity as prevailed in 1970). Assuming that the value of the posting intensity coefficient was a fixed percentage of the average price would yield a gain of $485 million for regular and $328 million for premium for a total of $813 million, as shown in Table 7.

Universal posting in 1970, then, would have resulted in an annual gain to consumers of $283 million ($607 million minus $324 million) over what a market as competitive as Los Angeles would

---

[35] *National Petroleum News: Factbook Issue,* vol. 68, no. 5A (mid-May 1976), pp. 88–89. Note that dollar benefits are calculated by first multiplying the percent of stations not posting and the posting intensity coefficient, after converting it to dollars, rounding this result to four places after the decimal, and then multiplying it by the number of gallons sold.

[36] Ibid., p. 6.

Table 5

CALCULATION OF CONSUMER BENEFITS DUE TO UNIVERSAL POSTING, AT 1970 PRICES AND CONSUMPTION LEVELS

	Leaded Regular	Leaded Premium
Percentage of stations not posting price, 1970	39%	47%
Number of gallons estimated sold, 1970[a]	51.2 billion	38.7 billion
Value of posting intensity of coefficient	−.94	−2.30
Consumer benefit due to increased posting intensity	(.39) ($.0094) (51.2 billion) = $(.0037) (51.2 billion) = $189 million	(.47) ($.0230) (38.7 billion) = $(.0108) (38.7 billion) = $418 million
Total consumer benefit, at 1970 prices and sales	$189 million +418 million $607 million	

[a] Gallons of regular and premium sold were estimated using the percent of regular and premium sales and the total number of gallons sold.

Table 6

CALCULATION OF CONSUMER BENEFITS DUE TO UNIVERSAL POSTING, AT 1970 PRICES AND 1975 CONSUMPTION LEVELS

	Leaded Regular	Leaded Premium
Percentage of stations not posting price, 1970	39%	47%
Number of gallons estimated sold, 1975[a]	83.7 billion	19.9 billion
Value of posting intensity coefficient	−.94	−2.30
Consumer benefit due to increased posting intensity	(.39) ($.0094) (83.7 billion) = $(.0037) (83.7 billion) = $310 million	(.47) ($.0230) (19.9 billion) = $(.0108) (19.9 billion) = $215 million
Total consumer benefit, at 1970 prices and 1975 sales	$310 million +215 million $525 million	

[a] Gallons of regular and premium sold were estimated using the percent of regular and premium sales and the total number of gallons sold.

Table 7

CALCULATION OF CONSUMER BENEFITS DUE TO UNIVERSAL POSTING, AT 1975 PRICES AND 1975 CONSUMPTION LEVELS

	Leaded Regular	Leaded Premium
Percentage of stations not posting price, 1970	39%	47%
Number of gallons estimated sold, 1975[a]	83.7 billion	19.9 billion
Estimated value of posting coefficient	−1.48	−3.52
Consumer benefit due to increased posting intensity	(.39) (.0148) (83.7 billion) = (.0058) (83.7 billion) = $485 million	(.47) (.0352) (19.9 billion) = (.0165) (19.9 billion) = $328 million
Total consumer benefit, at 1975 prices and 1975 sales	$485 million +328 million $813 million	

[a] Gallons of regular and premium sold were estimated using the percent of regular and premium sales and the total number of gallons sold.

have provided; in 1975 it would have resulted in a gain to consumers of from $203 million ($525 million minus $322 million) to $306 million ($813 million minus $507 million).

Further Benefits. The benefits described above are limited to gains that result from a reduced average level of prices; they do not include any gain that might result from a reduced dispersion of prices. Since posting is expected to reduce price dispersion and a reduction in price dispersion is expected to reduce the amount of search activity needed to find lower prices, the benefits of posting include the value of consumers' search time saved. Next, the impact of posting on price dispersion is analyzed in order to determine whether, as expected, an increase in posting intensity is likely to reduce search costs.

The dependent variable in this analysis is the coefficient of variation of the price of gasoline (the coefficient of variation is defined as the standard deviation of prices in a metropolitan area divided by the average price in the area). The sample size for the analysis thus becomes equal to seventeen, the number of different areas in the study (counting the four New York areas separately). Due to the large size of the New York area and the likely absence of competition among stations located in the four large subareas of New York, they have been included as separate areas with their own characteristics. This was done because the Lundberg data defined these subareas for New York but no other area and because the cost of creating a similar distinction for, say, Los Angeles was prohibitive. The coefficient of variation is calculated for both leaded regular and leaded premium prices for each metropolitan area. The independent variable is the proportion of stations in the area that post prices. The higher the proportion of stations that post prices, the lower is the dispersion of prices about the average expected to be (see Table 8).

The proportion of posting stations is, as expected, negatively and significantly related to the coefficient of variation for both grades. The proportion of explained variation in the dependent variable amounts to .29 in the case of leaded regular and .50 in the case of leaded premium (see Table 9). The impact of the proportion posting on the coefficient of variation can be illustrated with an example.

Suppose that the proportion posting leaded regular in an area were to increase from .61 (the proportion posting leaded regular for the entire sample, as reported in Table 1) to .90 (the proportion posting in the Los Angeles and Sacramento areas, the highest in any of the metropolitan areas in the sample). The increase in the proportion posting (.29) would result in a change in the coefficient of variation amounting to —.011 (.29 × —.039). Thus the average coefficient of variation for the nation would be reduced by 17 percent, from .058 to .047. In the case of leaded premium, if the proportion posting were to increase from .53 (the average proportion posting for the entire sample, as reported in Table 1) to .74 (the average proportion posting premium in the Los Angeles area, this being the second highest proportion posting of all the areas studied), the coefficient of variation would be reduced by .012(.21 × —.057). Thus the average coefficient of variation in leaded premium for the nation would be reduced by 24 percent, from .049 to .037. The standard deviation of the coefficient of variation is .021 and .018 for the leaded regular and leaded premium cases, respectively, so these reductions amount to between one-half and three-quarters of one standard deviation reduction in the coefficient of variation.

Although these estimates do not reveal the magnitude of the reduction in search costs that would be brought about by an increase in posting intensity, they do suggest that some reduction in these costs would be enjoyed. This cost saving would have to be added to the price saving described above in order to compute the total social benefits attributable to the increase in posting intensity.

Table 8
DATA USED IN PRICE VARIATION ANALYSIS

Area	Leaded Regular		Leaded Premium	
	Coefficient of variation	Proportion posting price	Coefficient of variation	Proportion posting price
Los Angeles	.044	.90	.035	.74
San Diego	.034	.72	.028	.53
Sacramento	.038	.90	.029	.77
Stockton	.037	.67	.027	.48
San Joaquin Valley	.035	.56	.028	.47
San Francisco	.039	.66	.031	.50
Phoenix	.053	.65	.041	.48
Tucson	.066	.70	.063	.50
Reno/Las Vegas	.094	.67	.081	.42
Seattle	.041	.77	.039	.59
Portland	.046	.69	.044	.52
Spokane	.089	.71	.058	.40
Boise	.068	.19	.073	.12
White Plains	.076	.10	.059	.06
New York City	.079	.01	.076	.01
New Jersey	.084	.29	.059	.23
Long Island	.072	.12	.062	.08

Table 9
PRICE VARIATION ANALYSIS

Variable	Leaded Regular			Leaded Premium		
	Mean value	Coefficient	t-value	Mean value	Coefficient	t-value
Proportion posting	.41	$-.057$	-3.71	.55	$-.039$	-2.37
Constant		.049			.080	
Coefficient of variation	.049			.058		
R^2	.50			.29		
F	14.79			6.23		
N (number of observations)	17			17		

Costs of Requiring Universal Posting

Some of the costs ascribable to price posting are reflected in federal and state laws that prohibit posting on aesthetic grounds. Federal law has prohibited signs of any kind within 700 feet of interstate highways (although recognition of the difficulties thereby created for travelers in search of food, lodging, and gas has led to the appearance of small signs indicating the brands available at interstate highway exits). The social costs of requiring posting would also include construction costs and enforcement costs.

The typical service station price sign costs between $65 and $300. Since there were approximately 222,000 service stations in the United States in 1970, and since only 61 percent of the stations in our sample posted regular prices and only 53 percent posted premium prices, universal posting would have cost from $5.2 million (79,920 times $65) to $23.9 million (79,920 times $300) for regular and $7.1 million (108,780 times $65) to $32.6 million (108,780 times $300) for premium. Since 85 percent of the stations not posting premium also did not post regular, however, these costs are not additive; since 15 percent of the stations not posting premium did post regular, only 15 percent of the $7.1 million to $32.6 million should be added to the cost of posting regular, bringing total costs to between $6.3 million and $28.8 million.

A sizable proportion of the signs would be erected voluntarily if there were as much competition in each area as in the Los Angeles areas. Only those signs that stations would not erect unless required to would need to be counted as social costs. In that case, as many as 90 percent of all stations might voluntarily post regular and 74 percent might voluntarily post premium prices. The costs of sign erection for the remaining 10 percent (22.2 thousand) to post regular would vary from $1.4 million to $6.6 million and for the remaining 26 percent to post premium would vary from $3.8 million to $17.3 million. Total construction costs would be estimated at between $2.0 million and $9.2 million.

There are costs that would be imposed upon the stations and society by requiring universal price posting. Not only would there be costs associated with the erection of the sign, but there would also be annual costs associated with enforcing the requirement. There may also be annual costs to be considered in developing and maintaining cost-minimizing, uniform criteria by which the signs are to be judged adequate. For example, the law that requires posting in Los Angeles states that the signs must be visible from all lanes of traffic on all adjacent streets. Whether the sign is visible, however, depends on how big the sign is, how far away the viewer is from the sign, and in which lane he is located, so that difficulty is encountered in enforcing this kind of requirement.

Since it is not possible at this time to place a dollar value on all the costs associated with requiring universal posting, it would appear more advisable to focus attention upon the benefits from the elimination of laws prohibiting price posting. Market forces will tend to produce an increase in posting intensity in such situations. Consumers will benefit. Society will not experience any of the regulatory costs that would be associated with requiring universal posting; such regulatory costs can be sizable and could be greater than the resulting benefits.

Summary

The focus of this study on the role of price advertising is unique. The findings in chapter 3 are consistent with the new approach to consumer demand theory, presented in chapter 2, that treats the time consumers spend searching for information as an alternative to work and leisure. According to this theory, price advertising increases the efficiency of search time for all consumers. With only a small investment in additional search for lower prices the typical consumer can find lower prices quite rapidly when prices are advertised. The result is that lower-price firms capture increased business from higher-price firms. Competition forces higher-price firms to cut their prices and forces out of business firms that are unable to cut their prices and still cover costs. In equilibrium, the average price will be lower, the spread of prices will be lower, and more efficient firms will have displaced less efficient firms. Finally, because of the reduced price dispersion, consumers will need to search less in this new environment.

Consumer gains throughout the nation in 1975 due to price posting as intense as that in the Los Angeles area were estimated to be at least $322 million annually and possibly as much as $507 million annually. The potential price savings due to universal price posting were estimated to be at least $525 million annually and possibly as much as $813 million annually. Consumer benefits in the form of reduced search costs ascribable to the reduced dispersion of prices associated with more frequent price posting were found to exist, although they could not be estimated.

4
CONCLUSIONS

There is a growing controversy over the consumer's benefits from advertising. Some argue that advertising primarily benefits advertisers by making it more difficult for small or newly entering firms to compete. The result, it is claimed, is excess profits for the firms already in an industry and little gain to consumers. Others argue that advertising eliminates excess profits by making consumers better informed. It is claimed that better informed consumers contribute to increased competition and thereby to lower prices.

Although existing studies offer mixed evidence on the effects of manufacturers' advertising on manufacturers' prices, they offer clearer evidence on the effects of such advertising on consumer prices. Manufacturers' advertising creates product identifiability, which makes consumer search and price comparison easier and hence helps reduce the markup or distribution margin between manufacturers and retailers.

The available evidence from previous studies also indicates that the quality of goods and services has no systematic association with whether or not prices are advertised. This tends to support the notion that price advertising increases competition and reduces prices without reducing quality. However, the available evidence on quality is meager at best.

This study focused on the benefits to consumers from retail price advertising. A form of advertising that conveys only product price information—the posting of the pump price of gasoline on large signs visible to the passing motorist—was examined for 1970. Consumer benefits in the form of price savings ascribable to posting everywhere as intensively as in the Los Angeles area were estimated at $322 million annually assuming model results based on 1970 prices and assuming gallonage sold in 1975. The gains estimated using the model results based on 1970 prices may not accurately reflect gains after the oil embargo caused gasoline prices to double; the 1975 gains could be as high as $507 million annually. Price savings ascribable to universal price posting were estimated at $525 million annually for gallonage in 1975, or an additional $203 million (525 — 322) beyond what a market as competitive as the Los Angeles area would have produced. These savings were estimated to be as high as $813 million annually, or an additional $306 million (813 — 507), if the doubling of gasoline prices had its assumed effect. Consumer benefits in the form of reduced search costs ascribable to the reduced dispersion of prices associated with more frequent price posting were found to exist, although they could not be estimated.

This study also found that the impact of price posting intensity tends to be greater among major-brand stations. The implication of this finding is that consumers act as though there is information value in knowing that a station offers a major rather than an independent brand. Thus, this study has found some support for the notion that manufacturers' advertising creates product identifiability and makes consumer search easier, thus reducing prices.

The initial purpose of this inquiry was to identify the net social losses due to laws prohibiting price posting. In the absence of any law prohibiting or requiring price posting the marketplace will determine some equilibrium intensity of posting. Since posting is usually quite intense where it is allowed, it seems evident that the marketplace yields a fairly high posting intensity in areas where it is permitted. A law prohibiting posting would cause a large change in posting intensity and would cause a substantial rise in prices and their dispersion. The estimated loss in benefits due to the absence of posting in the New York area alone amounts to at least $25.4 million annually. What is to be gained by prohibiting posting? The costs of sign erection appear to be small in comparison. Such laws prohibiting posting appear motivated more by profit than by aesthetics. Besides, the costs of sign erection are borne by the stations who, in areas where posting is allowed, evidently increase their profits by more than the cost of the sign. The principal externality that a law prohibiting posting would seem to eliminate is that consisting of the increased search efficiency arising from posting.

APPENDIXES

APPENDIX A

The consumer maximizes his utility function given by

$$U = U(x_i, l) \qquad (i = 1, \ldots, n) \qquad (1)$$

where U is definitionally single valued and at least twice continuously differentiable. The quantities of goods consumed (x_i) and the proportion of time spent in pure leisure (l) are the only arguments in the consumer's utility function.[1] The first- and second-order partial derivatives of U are denoted as follows

$$U_{x_i}, U_l, U_{x_i l}, U_{x_i x_i}, U_{ll}, \text{ and } U_{lx_i} \qquad (i = 1, \ldots, n).$$

The following assumptions concerning the partial derivatives of the utility function are made for the remainder of the derivation, unless specifically stated otherwise

$$U_{x_i} > 0, U_l > 0, U_{x_i x_i} < 0, U_{ll} < 0, U_{lx_i} > 0.$$

It is assumed that the consumer has two sources of income, wages from the sale of his labor time and nonwage income either from past investment or from windfall and losses. Thus income is a function of w_i, the wage rate that the consumer could get in the i-th occupation; h_i, the time that he spends in the i-th occupation;[2] and

---

[1] Search does not enter the utility function directly because it is assumed that the loss of utility due to increased search time is merely that utility lost from nonleisure of the same duration. Certainly, a case for directly including search in the utility function can be made (for example, some people may receive positive utility from "shopping"), but this particular modification is outside the scope of this discussion.

[2] Although it is recognized that overtime wages and wages from moonlighting in another occupation may be markedly different from wages in the consumer's primary occupation, a modification to include such differences would needlessly complicate the analysis.

α_j, the income obtained or lost from the j-th nonlabor activity. Note that α_j can be either negative or positive. For example, a lump-sum tax would reduce the consumer's income, whereas welfare payments would increase it. For simplicity, however, it is assumed that the consumer has already chosen an occupation in which he earns a constant wage rate w, no matter how long he works, and that all nonwage income is lumped together into α. The linear income function becomes

$$Y = wh + \alpha \tag{2}$$

where h is the chosen amount of work time. For the purpose of this study the simplifying linearity assumption does not occasion much loss in analytical content. Since the study is not concerned with the theory of job choice, the grouping of all occupations into one does not pose any problem. Therefore the consumer's budget constraint is given by

$$\sum_{i=1}^{n} p_i x_i = wh + \alpha \tag{3}$$

where p_i is the price paid for the i-th commodity x_i.

p_i is the price actually paid by the consumer; in this model it is not parametrically given to the consumer. Within limits, the consumer can alter the prices paid for commodities by searching (shopping around). Thus p_i is a function of the amount of time spent shopping for the i-th commodity.[3]

The price search function is given by

$$p_i = p_i(s_i | p_i^0, e_i) \tag{4}$$

where s_i is the time spent shopping for the i-th good, p_i^0 is the initial price of the i-th good given zero search time, and e indicates the search efficiency of the consumer. The function is assumed to be single valued and at least twice continuously differentiable. Further, over the relevant range p_i is a monotonically decreasing function of the time invested in the search for price information, that is, $\dfrac{\partial p_i}{\partial s_i} < 0$.

[3] Peterson and Mincer extended the search function to include the expenditure of money, as well as time, to aid in the search for prices. See R. L. Peterson, "The Time Cost of Goods (for the Poor)" (Southern Methodist University, unpublished manuscript, 1971); Jacob Mincer, "Market Prices, Opportunity Costs, and Income Effects," in *Measurement in Economics*, ed. C. F. Christ (Stanford, Calif.: Stanford University Press, 1963). For example, some price information can be gained by purchasing *Consumer Reports*, a publication of the Consumers Union of United States, a product testing and rating organization. However, since the scope of this study includes only the time cost of information gathering, a more complete investigation of the money-cost problems is left for others to explore.

It is further assumed that the return from search diminishes with increased search time, that is, $\frac{\partial^2 p_i}{\partial s^2} > 0$.[4]

Before proceeding further with the model, it is well to stop and describe what this particular search function implies about the world in which the consumer lives. In the first place, the search function is a single-period analytical device, implying a one-period model. In future periods $\frac{\partial p_i}{\partial s_i}$ would decrease as the consumer gains information during present price search, assuming that the world does not change drastically between periods. The consumer conducts the appropriate amount of search in the first period and in the process gains price information about future periods. Here the p_i^0's are rather like gasoline prices on the pump, catalog prices from a mail-order house, or window prices on automobiles. The consumer does not expect these basic prices to change much over several periods in his short-run planning horizon. He does know that he need pay no price higher than p_i^0 for x_i, and he believes that if he spends some time searching, the price actually paid will be lower than p_i^0. How much lower, he feels, depends upon the amount of time spent searching, even though the consumer knows that an additional unit of search does not always reduce price. At the beginning of the period he does think that price is inversely related to search in the way given by equation (4). Therefore, the search function used here is related to a planning period and not to the actual process of search.

The complete budget constraint is thus

$$\sum_{i=1}^{n} p_i x_i = \sum_{i=1}^{n} p_i(s_i | p_i^0, e) x_i = wh + \alpha. \tag{5}$$

The consumer's time constraint is defined as

$$T \equiv \sum_{i=1}^{n} s_i + l + h \tag{6}$$

where T is the total amount of time available in the time period under consideration. In this model the budget and time constraints

4 Solow (see George J. Stigler, "The Economics of Information," *Journal of Political Economy*, vol. 49, no. 3 [June 1961], p. 215, footnote 4) has shown that for any stable distribution of prices the minimum expected price from a random sample of searches decreases at a decreasing rate as the number of searches increases. Thus

$$\frac{\partial^2 p_i}{\partial s_i^2} > 0.$$

are considered separately, even though the time constraint could be substituted into the budget constraint.[5] The resulting Lagrange expression to be maximized is

$$L = U(x_1, \ldots, x_n, l) + \lambda_1 \left(\sum_{i=1}^{n} p_i(s_i | p_i^0, e) x_i - hw - \alpha \right) \tag{7}$$

$$+ \lambda_2 \left(T - \sum_{i=1}^{n} s_i - l - h \right)$$

$$\frac{\partial L}{\partial x_i} = U_i + \lambda_1 p_i = 0 \qquad (i = 1, 2, \ldots, n) \tag{8}$$

$$\frac{\partial L}{\partial l} = U_l - \lambda_2 = 0 \tag{9}$$

$$\frac{\partial L}{\partial s_i} = \lambda_1 x_i \frac{\partial p_i}{\partial s_i} - \lambda_2 = 0 \qquad (i = 1, 2, \ldots, n) \tag{10}$$

$$\frac{\partial L}{\partial h} = -\lambda_1 w - \lambda_2 = 0 \tag{11}$$

$$\frac{\partial L}{\partial \lambda_1} = \sum_{i=1}^{n} p_i x_i - wh - \alpha = 0 \tag{12}$$

$$\frac{\partial L}{\partial \lambda_2} = T - \sum_{i=1}^{n} s_i - l - h = 0. \tag{13}$$

Second order conditions require that the matrix

$$H = \begin{bmatrix} U_{ij} & U_{il} & \lambda_1 \dfrac{\partial p_i}{\partial s_i} & 0 & p_i & 0 \\ U_{lj} & U_{ll} & 0 & 0 & 0 & -1 \\ \lambda_1 \dfrac{\partial p_i}{\partial s_i} & 0 & \lambda_1 x_i \dfrac{\partial^2 p_i}{\partial s_i^2} & 0 & x_i \dfrac{\partial p_i}{\partial x_i} & -1 \\ 0 & 0 & 0 & 0 & -w & -1 \\ p_i & 0 & x_i \dfrac{\partial p_i}{\partial s_i} & -w & 0 & 0 \\ 0 & -1 & -1 & -1 & 0 & 0 \end{bmatrix} \quad (i, j = 1, \ldots, n) \tag{14}$$

be associated with a negative definite quadratic form.

[5] By the continued separation of the budget and time constraints, this model explicitly incorporates Becker's suggestion that the indirect (time) costs be treated on the same footing as the costs of market goods. See Gary S. Becker, "A Theory of the Allocation of Time," *Economic Journal*, vol. 75 (September 1965), pp. 493-517.

The first-order conditions make up a system of $2n + 4$ unknowns $x_1 \ldots x_n$, l, s_1, $\ldots$, s_n, h, λ_1, λ_2). This system of equations determines the optimal solution values for the unknowns as functions of the exogenous variables. Solving the system and using the inverse function theorem obtains

$$x_i = x_i(p_i^0, \ldots, p_n^0, e, w, \alpha) \qquad (i = 1, \ldots, n)$$

$$s_i = s_i(p_i^0, \ldots, p_n^0, e, w, \alpha) \qquad (i = 1, \ldots, n)$$

$$h = h(p_i^0, \ldots, p_n^0, e, w, \alpha) \qquad (i = 1, \ldots, n)$$

$$l = l(p_i^0, \ldots, p_n^0, e, w, \alpha) \qquad (i = 1, \ldots, n).$$

(15)

Economic Interpretation of First-Order Conditions

The economic interpretation of the equilibrium conditions set forth in equations (8) through (13) is fairly straightforward. Equation (8) gives the conventional condition for utility maximization: additional amounts of a commodity are purchased until the marginal utility of the commodity is proportional to the commodity price, the factor of proportionality being the marginal utility of income,

$$\frac{U_i}{p_i} = -\lambda_1 \qquad (i = 1, \ldots, n).$$

(16)

From equation (9), the marginal utility of leisure U_l equals the marginal utility of an additional unit of time, λ_2. Or, by solving equations (10) and (11) for λ_2 and substituting the solutions into equation (9)

$$\frac{U_l}{w} = -\lambda_1$$

(17)

and

$$\frac{U_l}{-x_i \dfrac{\partial p_i}{\partial s_i}} = -\lambda_1 \qquad (i = 1, 2, \ldots, n).$$

(18)

Here, as in other demand-for-leisure models, the price of leisure is the return obtained through the next best alternative, work, and the return to work is the wage rate. In line with this, equation (17) shows that the consumer takes leisure until the marginal utility of leisure is proportional to its price w. In this model, however, there is another alternative for the consumer's time: search for more information about lower prices. Therefore, the price of leisure is also the consumer's expected saving from an additional unit of time expended in search for lower prices. By searching for more information about prices before making his final purchases, *ceteris paribus*, the consumer believes he will find successively lower prices. The consumer may thus indirectly increase his utility from search by taking advantage of his new ability to buy more goods at the lower prices. In equation (10), since x_i (a positive quantity) is the quantity of the commodity he wishes to purchase and $\dfrac{\partial p_i}{\partial s_i}$ (a negative number) is the expected reduction in price obtained through his search efforts, $-x_i \dfrac{\partial p_i}{\partial s_i}$ is the positive saving (or return) expected from additional search.[6] From equation (18) it is clear the consumer will maximize his utility when the marginal utility of leisure is proportional to the return from search, the factor of proportionality again being the marginal utility of income. The wage rate is thus but one price of leisure, the other being the return to another use of time: search. Since all prices of leisure equal $\dfrac{U_l}{\lambda_1}$, all are equal in equilibrium.[7]

Combining equations (8) and (10), one obtains

$$\frac{U_i}{p_i} = \frac{U_j}{p_j} = \frac{U_l}{w} = \frac{U_l}{-x_i \dfrac{\partial p_i}{\partial s_i}} = \frac{U_l}{-x_j \dfrac{\partial p_j}{\partial s_j}} = -\lambda_1 \qquad (19)$$

as a short description of the first-order conditions for constrained utility maximization.

The marginal utility of leisure must bear the same relation to the wage rate and the return to search as the marginal utility of each commodity bears to the price of that commodity.

From equation (19) it is clear that

$$p_i x_i \left(\frac{\dfrac{\partial p_i}{\partial s_i}}{p_i} \right) = p_j x_j \left(\frac{\dfrac{\partial p_j}{\partial s_j}}{p_j} \right) \qquad (20)$$

---

[6] The saving from a marginal unit of search in this model, $-x_i \dfrac{\partial p_i}{\partial s_i}$, is strictly compatible with the saving in Stigler's model, $q \left| \dfrac{\partial p}{\partial s} \right|$. In each model, the saving is the quantity of the commodity demanded multiplied by the reduction in price. Any differences arising from the use of "absolute value" or "minus sign" notation affect neither the economic interpretation nor the validity of either model.

[7] This conclusion is analogous to the conclusion in production theory that all factors of production have the same value in all uses.

where $\dfrac{\frac{\partial p_i}{\partial s_i}}{p_i}$ is the proportional variation in price expected from addi-

tional search, evaluated at a particular price. From equation (20), the expected variation in the price of a good is inversely related to the expenditure ($p_i x_i$) on that good, relative to the equilibrium position of other goods. That is, in equilibrium, when the consumer is spending more on x_i than on $x_j (p_i x_i > p_j x_j)$, the proportional variation in x_j must exceed the proportional variation in x_i so that

$$\left(\frac{\frac{\partial p_i}{\partial s_i}}{p_i} \right) < \left(\frac{\frac{\partial p_j}{\partial s_j}}{p_j} \right). \tag{21}$$

If the greater expenditure upon x_i occurs because the quantity of it consumed is greater than the quantity of x_j consumed, prices equal, then the marginal price returns from search for x_i are less than the marginal price returns from search for $x_j \left(\dfrac{\partial p_i}{\partial s_i} < \dfrac{\partial p_j}{\partial s_j} \right)$. Since equal search functions for the two goods were assumed and there are diminishing marginal returns from search $\left(\dfrac{\partial^2 p_i}{\partial s_i{}^2} < 0 \right)$ analysis of equation (21) reveals that the consumer searches longer the greater the expenditure on the commodity.

Use of an Aggregate Commodity

Even though much information can be gained by considering an n-commodity bundle with n separate search functions, the goods-time and the leisure-work-search trade-offs in the consumer's consumption bundle may be more readily understood by grouping the commodities into a single commodity, denoted by x.[8] With a utility function

---

[8] The comparative statics approach in this model is too complex to allow suffi-cient concentration on the goods-time trade-off. For instance, a change in the price of x_i will change the prices of all other goods (relative to x_i) and perhaps cause a complete reorganization of the consumer's consumption bundle—an effect not directly necessary to determine work, leisure, and search. In this model, it is therefore assumed that if the price of one good changes, the prices of all other goods change in the same proportion and in the same direction. Since if the prices of a group of goods change in the same proportion, that group of goods behaves as if it were a single commodity, the bundle of goods consumed in this model may be considered to be a single (aggregate) com-modity. For this aggregate commodity, price index p has been assigned, the precise nature of which is not considered important for this model.

$U = U(x,l)$ and a single price-search function $p = p(s, p^0, e)$,[9] equilibrium conditions (8) through (13) are now

$$U_x + \lambda_1 p = 0 \tag{22}$$

$$U_l - \lambda_2 = 0 \tag{23}$$

$$\lambda_1 x \frac{\partial p}{\partial s} - \lambda_2 = 0 \tag{24}$$

$$-\lambda_1 w - \lambda_2 = 0 \tag{25}$$

$$px - wh - \alpha = 0 \tag{26}$$

$$T - s - l - h = 0. \tag{27}$$

These first-order conditions are analyzed exactly like those in the n-commodity models. The advantage of the one-good model is the relative simplicity of the comparative statics as compared to the more complex model.

Search Efficiency

An increase in search efficiency could originate from either the supply side or the demand side of the market. On the supply side, a rash of price wars by gasoline stations would imply a fall in the prices that searching consumers could expect to find. In this event search efficiency would vary with changes in the commodity price. But a change in search efficiency could also come about through "learning" by the consumer. For instance, as the consumer searches more and more, he learns which service stations usually have higher prices and which have lower prices and thus how to avoid wasteful search. As consumers learn more about products, say, as a result of advertising, they presumably acquire the ability to search more efficiently.

To isolate the effects of a change in search efficiency, an efficiency shift parameter e has been added to the price search function in equation (4). An exogenous increase in search efficiency has the effect of lowering the final price of the commodity, *ceteris paribus*. Since this section concentrates on an exogenous change in efficiency, it is initially assumed that the change in search efficiency has no effect on the marginal price returns to search, so that $\frac{\partial^2 p}{\partial s \partial e} = 0$.

[9] This search function is the same as the search function specified earlier, with one exception. Search time s is an aggregate search time such that it is the total search undertaken for all commodities together. As with price p, if search time changes for one commodity, it changes for the others in the same proportion and in the same direction.

Although it may appear more "realistic" for $\frac{\partial^2 p}{\partial s \partial e} < 0$,[10] it will be shown that basically the same results can be obtained using the simpler assumption of $\frac{\partial^2 p}{\partial s \partial e} = 0$. A change in efficiency under the condition $\frac{\partial^2 p}{\partial s \partial e} = 0$ might occur when each retail seller, because of an industrywide cost reduction, reduces price by a certain amount (say, by the amount of the industrywide cost reduction). Gasoline initially selling for 69.9 cents at one station and 67.9 cents at another might sell for 68.9 cents and 66.9 cents at the two, respectively, after the change in prices. This case is analogous to a change in initial commodity price that does not affect the marginal price return to search.

In order to determine the effects on the consumer's behavior of a change in search efficiency, one displaces the equilibrium conditions with respect to the search efficiency parameter e and obtains, in matrix form,

$$[D] \begin{bmatrix} \dfrac{dx}{de} \\[2mm] \dfrac{dl}{de} \\[2mm] \dfrac{ds}{de} \\[2mm] \dfrac{dh}{de} \\[2mm] \dfrac{d\lambda_1}{de} \\[2mm] \dfrac{d\lambda_2}{de} \end{bmatrix} = \begin{bmatrix} -\lambda_1 \dfrac{\partial p}{\partial e} \\[2mm] 0 \\[2mm] 0 \\[2mm] 0 \\[2mm] -x \dfrac{\partial p}{\partial e} \\[2mm] 0 \end{bmatrix} \qquad (28)$$

---

[10] $\frac{\partial^2 p}{\partial s \partial e} < 0$ says that the marginal reduction in price from a marginal increase in search time will be greater the greater the search efficiency. For example, consider the consumer who, through n searches, finds a price reduction of ten dollars. If he were suddenly more efficient, the reduction in price might be fifteen dollars for n searches. Thus the change in marginal price return from ten dollars to fifteen dollars for n searches increases the absolute value of the marginal price return ($\left|\frac{\partial p}{\partial s}\right|$) but, since $\frac{\partial p}{\partial s} < 0$, decreases (makes more negative) the marginal price return.

Solving by Cramer's rule, the following results are obtained

$$\frac{dx}{de} = -x\frac{\partial p}{\partial e}\frac{D_{51}}{D} - \lambda_1\frac{\partial p}{\partial e}\frac{D_{11}}{D} \tag{29}$$

$$\frac{dl}{de} = -x\frac{\partial p}{\partial e}\frac{D_{52}}{D} - \lambda_1\frac{\partial p}{\partial e}\frac{D_{12}}{D} \tag{30}$$

$$\frac{ds}{de} = -x\frac{\partial p}{\partial e}\frac{D_{53}}{D} - \lambda_1\frac{\partial p}{\partial e}\frac{D_{13}}{D} \tag{31}$$

$$\frac{dh}{de} = -x\frac{\partial p}{\partial e}\frac{D_{54}}{D} - \lambda_1\frac{\partial p}{\partial e}\frac{D_{14}}{D}. \tag{32}$$

Before these equations can be discussed it is necessary to explain more fully the relation of search efficiency to the price of leisure. Recall that the wage rate and the return to search are both prices of leisure. A change in the wage rate directly affects only the amount of goods the consumer is able to buy. However, a change in search efficiency not only affects the amount of goods a consumer can buy, but does so by influencing the final price the consumer pays for his goods. A change in the price of leisure due to a change in search efficiency is in this way different from a change in the price of leisure due to a change in the wage rate.

Since the price of leisure increases (decreases) as the search efficiency increases (decreases), one expects an "income effect" and a "substitution effect." Equations (30) and (32) reflect exactly these effects. With $\frac{D_{5j}}{D}$ the effect of a change in pure income, $-x\frac{\partial p}{\partial e}\frac{D_{5j}}{D}$ is the income effect for each variable of a change in search efficiency. The income effect due to a change in search efficiency is positive for normal commodities; positive for leisure, if leisure is normal; positive for search; and negative for work if leisure is normal. Take, for example, the case of a consumer who has already allocated his time between search, work, and leisure in an optimal distribution. Before actually carrying out his intentions, however, the consumer receives a windfall income. His initial budget is now greater by exactly the amount of his windfall gain. With a greater purchasing power, he will buy more x and spend more time searching for lower prices of these additional goods. Able to buy more with less work, the consumer works less and takes more leisure. This conclusion has intuitive appeal because, after income has increased, the value of the consumer's work time is less, relative to his total income, than it was before the increase. Thus

$$-x\frac{\partial p}{\partial e}\frac{D_{51}}{D} > 0 \qquad\qquad (33)$$

$$-x\frac{\partial p}{\partial e}\frac{D_{52}}{D} > 0 \qquad\qquad (34)$$

$$-x\frac{\partial p}{\partial e}\frac{D_{53}}{D} > 0 \qquad\qquad (35)$$

$$-x\frac{\partial p}{\partial e}\frac{D_{54}}{D} < 0. \qquad\qquad (36)$$

In equation (29), the second term on the right side, $-\lambda_1\frac{\partial p}{\partial e}\frac{D_{11}}{D}$, represents the substitution effect for a change in search efficiency. Since the successive bordered principal minors of D must alternate in sign, $\frac{D_{11}}{D} < 0$; hence

$$-\lambda_1\frac{\partial p}{\partial e}\frac{D_{11}}{D} > 0. \qquad\qquad (37)$$

Analysis of equation (29) reveals that the signs of the substitution and income effects are positive for normal goods. Thus, as search efficiency increases, more goods are consumed.

The second term in equation (30) represents the substitution effect for leisure; by expansion, the second term is found to be negative. If leisure is normal, from equations (34) and (30), an increase in search efficiency will increase or decrease time spent in leisure according to whether the income effect is greater than or less than the substitution effect.

By expansion, the second term in equation (31) is found to be positive. Since both the income effect and substitution effect are positive, an increase in search efficiency has the effect of always increasing the amount of time spent in search. Thus, regardless of the income level of the consumer or the slope of his labor supply curve, an increase in search efficiency will prompt him to spend more time in his relatively more rewarding endeavor, search.

The substitution effect on work due to a change in search efficiency cannot be readily signed. By expansion, the second term in equation (32) is found to be composed of several positive and negative terms, the relative magnitudes of which are mathematically indeterminate. However, economic analysis reveals that the sign of this substitution effect is negative. An increase in search efficiency, quite apart from having an income effect on work,[11] changes the relative prices of work and search. As search efficiency increases, the marginal return to search is greater than the marginal return to work: the consumer substitutes the more rewarding search time for his less rewarding work time. Thus, the substitution effect on work of a change in search efficiency is negative. Since both the income and substitution effect on work are negative, an increase in search efficiency will decrease time spent working.

There are several conclusions that may, in summary, be drawn about the effect of a change in search efficiency on work, leisure, and search. If a change in search efficiency has no effect on the marginal price returns to search, so that $\frac{\partial^2 p}{\partial s \partial e} = 0$, and if the income effect dominates the substitution effect, then an increase in search efficiency will induce the consumer to search more, enjoy more leisure, and work less. If, however, the change in search efficiency has an effect on the marginal price return to search ($\frac{\partial^2 p}{\partial s \partial e} \neq 0$), then further analysis must be made.

In order to analyze a change in search efficiency that increases the marginal price returns to search such that $\frac{\partial^2 p}{\partial s \partial e} < 0$, one displaces the equilibrium conditions with respect to the search efficiency parameter e and obtains, in matrix form,

$$[D] \begin{bmatrix} \dfrac{dx}{de} \\[2mm] \dfrac{dl}{de} \\[2mm] \dfrac{ds}{de} \\[2mm] \dfrac{dh}{de} \\[2mm] \dfrac{d\lambda_1}{de} \\[2mm] \dfrac{d\lambda_2}{de} \end{bmatrix} = \begin{bmatrix} -\lambda_1 \dfrac{\partial p}{\partial e} \\[2mm] 0 \\[2mm] -\lambda_1 x \dfrac{\partial^2 p}{\partial s \partial e} \\[2mm] 0 \\[2mm] -x \dfrac{\partial p}{\partial e} \\[2mm] 0 \end{bmatrix} \qquad (38)$$

---

[11] The income effect stems from the fact that at lower prices the consumer is able to buy more goods, *ceteris paribus*.

Solving by Cramer's rule, one obtains

$$\frac{dx}{de} = -x\frac{\partial p}{\partial e}\frac{D_{51}}{D} - \lambda_1\left[\frac{\partial p}{\partial e}\frac{D_{11}}{D} + x\frac{\partial^2 p}{\partial s\partial e}\frac{D_{31}}{D}\right] \qquad (39)$$

$$\frac{dl}{de} = -x\frac{\partial p}{\partial e}\frac{D_{52}}{D} - \lambda_1\left[\frac{\partial p}{\partial e}\frac{D_{12}}{D} + x\frac{\partial^2 p}{\partial s\partial e}\frac{D_{32}}{D}\right] \qquad (40)$$

$$\frac{ds}{de} = -x\frac{\partial p}{\partial e}\frac{D_{53}}{D} - \lambda_1\left[\frac{\partial p}{\partial e}\frac{D_{13}}{D} + x\frac{\partial^2 p}{\partial s\partial e}\frac{D_{33}}{D}\right] \qquad (41)$$

$$\frac{dh}{de} = -x\frac{\partial p}{\partial e}\frac{D_{54}}{D} - \lambda_1\left[\frac{\partial p}{\partial e}\frac{D_{14}}{D} + x\frac{\partial^2 p}{\partial s\partial e}\frac{D_{34}}{D}\right]. \qquad (42)$$

Note that equations (39) through (42) are the same as equations (29) through (32) with the exception of one extra term. The differences in substitution effects between the two sets of equations are attributable to the additional assumption that changes in search efficiency affect the marginal price returns to search. By expansion,

$$-\lambda_1 x\frac{\partial^2 p}{\partial s\partial e}\frac{D_{31}}{D} > 0 \qquad (43)$$

$$-\lambda_1 x\frac{\partial^2 p}{\partial s\partial e}\frac{D_{32}}{D} < 0 \qquad (44)$$

$$-\lambda_1 x\frac{\partial^2 p}{\partial s\partial e}\frac{D_{33}}{D} > 0 \qquad (45)$$

$$-\lambda_1 x\frac{\partial^2 p}{\partial s\partial e}\frac{D_{34}}{D} < 0. \qquad (46)$$

Analysis of equation (39) is straightforward and yields the same conclusion as the assumption $\frac{\partial^2 p}{\partial s\partial e} = 0$. Since from equations (43) and (37) the substitution effect is positive, and since x is a normal good such that the income effect is positive, an increase in search efficiency induces the consumer to buy more x. Intuitively, as the consumer becomes more efficient, he is able to buy more goods with no more work and no additional sacrifice of leisure because the prices of goods have fallen relative to the price of leisure and have fallen absolutely as well.

Equation (40) yields the same conclusion as the assumption $\frac{\partial^2 p}{\partial s\partial e} = 0$. From equation (44), the substitution effect on leisure of an increase in the marginal price reductions is negative. Since the substitution effect of an increase in search efficiency, which did not affect marginal price reductions, is also negative, the total substitution effect of an increase in search efficiency is negative. Intuitively, with the increase in search efficiency, search and work are relatively more rewarding uses of time: the price of leisure is greater. With a higher price of leisure, the substitution effect is negative. Thus the change in leisure from a change in search efficiency depends upon the relative strengths of the (positive) income effect and the (negative) substitution effect.

Equation (41) reveals that all three terms are positive: the income and substitution effects act in the same direction. An increase in search efficiency increases the return to search, making search relatively more rewarding than either work or leisure. Thus, for an increase in search efficiency, the consumer devotes even more time to search than formerly.

Equation (42) reveals that, as in equation (32), the substitution effect on work of a change in search efficiency is negative. That is, as the consumer becomes more efficient in search, the return to search becomes greater than the wage rate: the price of work increases. At a higher relative price of work, the consumer substitutes search time for the less valuable work time, thus decreasing work. Since the income effect and substitution effect are of the same sign, an increase in search efficiency has the effect of unambiguously decreasing work time.

Analysis of equations (29) through (32) and (39) through (42) reveals an interesting conclusion about the effects of assuming $\frac{\partial^2 p}{\partial s \partial e} = 0$ and $\frac{\partial^2 p}{\partial s \partial e} < 0$. If the increase in search efficiency affects the marginal price returns to search, the increase in goods, increase in search, and decrease in work will all be greater than if marginal price returns were not affected.[12] An increase in search efficiency that operates in two different ways, but in the same direction, would be expected to produce mutually reinforcing results. Any different results would be suspect. Thus, since both approaches yield essentially the same results, the rule of Occam's razor suggests the use of the assumption that marginal price returns to search are not affected by changes in efficiency.

---

[12] This analysis, while certainly applicable to the changes in leisure, does not yield such a neat interpretation. If the substitution effect dominates, then the increase in search efficiency that affects the marginal price returns will induce the consumer to increase leisure, but the increase will be less than if the change in search efficiency did not affect the marginal price return to search.

Conclusion

Analysis of equations (29) through (32) and (39) through (42) has shown that, regardless of the two definitions of search efficiency, an increase in search efficiency always induces the consumer initially to spend more time in search. The intuitive appeal is obvious because the consumer is more efficient at search, yet he has the same cost of time. The increase in efficiency will induce the consumer to buy additional normal goods, even though the consumer works fewer hours. The change in leisure due to a change in search efficiency will depend upon the relative strengths of the income and substitution effects.

With a positive correlation of prices from period to period, the lowest price found in one period will be the highest price the consumer must pay in the next. At the start of the next period, the consumer can buy the same bundle he bought in the prior period, but *without having to search at all*. However, if he searches some, but less than he did in the prior period, he can buy even more goods and have more leisure than before. With normal goods, this is what he will do. Another factor that will reduce the consumer's search time in subsequent periods arises from the market as a result of search by many consumers: higher-price sellers will face a dampened demand for their product and, accordingly, lower prices, thus reducing the spread of prices and also the returns to search. As has been seen, the lower the returns to search, the less consumers will search, *ceteris paribus*. The limiting case is, of course, when the consumer ultimately finds the lowest price that suppliers are willing to take for their commodity: any further search would yield no lower prices and hence would be wasteful. In this case, the consumer would be in the standard theoretical world of given, equal commodity prices.

APPENDIX B

The selection of Lundberg data was dictated by two considerations: first, a large sample was to be selected, so that stations for which the data could be obtained at the lowest possible price were to be included; second, stations that would provide a full range of observations on price posting were to be included. Thus stations from such areas as New York City or Boston where price posting was prohibited along with stations from such areas as Los Angeles where price posting was very common were to be included in the selection. Table B-1 provides a detailed description of the sample of stations resulting from these considerations.

The survey data are assembled by Lundberg in a manner that makes processing them difficult to analyze. The record created for each individual station contained four price fields for the different grades of gasoline sold. The first price field did not contain only the information for one grade, however. It appears as though the first price field was filled with whatever grade of gasoline was the lowest priced at the station; subsequent fields were filled with grades in ascending price order. The different patterns of price information in the entire sample resulting from this practice are displayed in Table B-6. As is evident from this table, the most frequent pattern is regular and then premium grade in the first and second positions, respectively, followed by regular, midgrade, and premium in the first three positions. Of 16,671 stations, 984 sold premium but did not sell regular grade, and 74 sold regular but did not sell premium grade. Because our regression analysis included only those stations selling both regular and premium grades, the 1,058 stations selling only one grade or the other were excluded.

Table B-1
SAMPLE SIZE BY AREA SAMPLED

Los Angeles Area: 6,336 Stations Sampled

Anaheim	101	Lakewood	123
Arcadia	95	Long Beach	64
Arlington	61	Lynwood	141
Beverly Hills	105	Montebello	144
Buena Park	193	Northridge	149
Burbank	158	Norwalk	112
Canoga Park	139	Ontario	112
Chinatown	144	Palos Verdes	25
Corona	42	Pasadena	213
Costa Mesa	59	Pomona	115
Covina	90	Redlands	67
Culver City	202	Redondo Beach	107
Cypress	95	Riverside	74
Downey	131	San Bernardino	154
East Los Angeles	55	San Clemente	31
East Whittier	38	San Pedro	28
El Monte	321	Santa Ana	212
El Segundo	39	Santa Monica	87
Fontana	91	Seal Beach	27
Fullerton	89	Signal Hill	89
Gardena	261	Tujunga	62
Glendale	116	Van Nuys	363
Hemet	16	Venice	109
Hollywood	267	Vernon	146
Huntington Beach	36	Watts	65
Inglewood	176	Westminster	104
La Habra	44	Whittier	73
Laguna Beach	63	Wilmington	113

San Diego Area: 772 Stations Sampled

Chula Vista	103	La Mesa	308
Clairemont	61	San Diego Beach Area	64
El Cajon	102	San Diego Downtown	134

Sacramento Area: 572 Stations Sampled

Carmichael	103	Sacramento East	37
North Highlands	28	Sacramento South	71
North Sacramento	40	Sacramento West	66
Orangevale	101	Southeast Sacramento	66
Rancho Cordova	26	West Sacramento	34

Table B-1 (continued)

Stockton Area: 326 Stations Sampled

Lodi	49	Stockton	143
Modesto	118	Tracy	16

San Joaquin Valley Area: 629 Stations Sampled

Bakersfield	282	Fresno	347

San Francisco Area: 2,548 Stations Sampled

Alameda	154	Redwood City	126
Bayview	28	Richmond District	31
Berkeley	32	Richmond Downtown	45
Burlingame	67	San Francisco Downtown	10
Campbell	190	San Francisco Fillmore	30
Daly City/Mission	132	San Francisco South of Market Street	30
Eastshore	38	San Francisco Twin Peaks	18
Fremont	45	San Jose	109
Livermore	46	San Jose East	81
Los Gatos	17	San Leandro	188
Marina	54	San Pablo	109
Mount Diablo	173	San Rafael	119
Oakland	107	South San Francisco	100
Palo Alto	100	Sunnyvale	107
Palo Alto North	76	Sunset/Westlake	73
Pittsburg	37	Vallejo	76

Phoenix Area: 830 Stations Sampled

Chandler	25	Phoenix North 2	44
Glendale	91	Phoenix North 3	86
Mesa	82	Phoenix South	45
Phoenix 1	172	Scottsdale	123
Phoenix 2	15	Sun City	15
Phoenix 3	21	Tempe	40
Phoenix North 1	71		

Tucson Area: 330 Stations Sampled

Tucson 1	52	Tucson 4	72
Tucson 2	38	Tucson 5	83
Tucson 3	48	Tucson 6	37

Reno/Las Vegas Area: 359 Stations Sampled

Henderson	22	Las Vegas South	42
Las Vegas Central	93	Reno/Sparks	151
Las Vegas North	51		

Table B-1 (continued)

Seattle Area: 1,516 Stations Sampled

Auburn	193	Olympia	51
Bellevue	125	Seattle North	336
Everett	97	Seattle South	294
Lynnwood	160	Tacoma	260

Portland Area: 1,143 Stations Sampled

Beaverton	71	Oregon City	46
Canby	37	Portland Downtown	60
Gresham	59	Portland East	167
Hillsboro	43	Portland North	215
Lake Oswego	22	Powell Valley	32
Longview	73	Ridgefield	15
Milwaukie	151	Tigard	56
Mulino	17	Vancouver	79

Spokane Area: 358 Stations Sampled

Cheney	20	Spokane North	102
Opportunity	70	Spokane Northwest	61
Spokane Downtown	76	Spokane South	29

Boise Area: 192 Stations Sampled

Boise	128	Nampa	35
Caldwell	29		

White Plains Area: 595 Stations Sampled

Bronx County	162	Lower Westchester	216
Fairfield	139	Upper Westchester	78

New York City Area: 677 Stations Sampled

Great Neck	36	Queens	140
Hempstead	93	Valley Stream	242
New York 1	166		

New Jersey Area: 658 Stations Sampled

Essex	202	Morris	95
Hudson	120	Union	241

Long Island Area: 1,443 Stations Sampled

Babylon	207	Islip	109
Baldwin	124	Oceanside	11
Glen Cove	143	Oyster Bay	200
Hampton Beach	96	Patchoque	135
Hicksville	197	Smithtown	106
Huntington	115		

Table B-2

DISTRIBUTION OF PRICES:
LOS ANGELES v. NEW YORK, LEADED REGULAR

Price (¢ per gallon)	Frequency	
	Los Angeles	New York
25	.001	0
26	.004	0
27	.005	.002
28	.006	.004
29	.003	.012
30	.001	.018
31	.012	.029
32	.039	.049
33	.131	.081
34	.147	.095
35	.476	.110
36	.164	.128
37	.007	.188
38	.001	.165
39	.001	.068
40	0	.028
41	.001	.013
42	0	.005
43	0	.001
44	0	.001
45	0	.001

Table B-3

DISTRIBUTION OF PRICES:
LOS ANGELES v. NEW YORK, LEADED PREMIUM

Price (¢ per gallon)	Frequency	
	Los Angeles	New York
29	.001	.002
30	.002	.003
31	.004	.012
32	.003	.019
33	.002	.023

Table B-3 (continued)

| Price | Frequency | |
(¢ per gallon)	Los Angeles	New York
34	.002	.047
35	.008	.061
36	.030	.076
37	.099	.103
38	.113	.115
39	.581	.179
40	.142	.176
41	.007	.099
42	.002	.050
43	.001	.022
44	0	.008
45	.001	.002
46	0	.001
47	0	.001
48	0	0
49	0	0

Table B-4

STANDARDIZED DISTRIBUTION OF PRICES: LOS ANGELES v. NEW YORK, LEADED REGULAR

$\frac{P-\bar{p}^a}{Sp}$	Frequency Los Angeles	$\frac{P-\bar{p}^a}{Sp}$	Frequency New York
− 6.86	.001		
− 6.13	.004	− 3.34	.002
− 5.40	.005	− 2.96	.004
− 4.67	.006	− 2.58	.012
− 3.94	.003	− 2.20	.018
− 3.21	.001	− 1.82	.029
− 2.48	.012	− 1.44	.049
− 1.75	.039	− 1.06	.081
− 1.02	.131	− 0.68	.095
− 0.29	.147	− 0.30	.110
0.44	.476	0.08	.128
1.17	.164	0.45	.188
1.90	.007	0.83	.165

$\dfrac{P-\bar{p}^{\,a}}{Sp}$	Frequency Los Angeles	$\dfrac{P-\bar{p}^{\,a}}{Sp}$	Frequency New York
2.63	.001	1.21	.068
3.36	.001	1.59	.028
4.09	0	1.97	.013
4.82	.001	2.35	.005
		2.73	.001
		3.11	.001
		3.49	.001

a Actual price minus the mean of prices divided by the standard deviation of prices.

Table B-5
STANDARDIZED DISTRIBUTION OF PRICES: LOS ANGELES v. NEW YORK, LEADED PREMIUM

$\dfrac{P-\bar{p}^{\,a}}{Sp}$	Frequency Los Angeles	$\dfrac{P-\bar{p}^{\,a}}{Sp}$	Frequency New York
-7.16	.001	-3.36	.002
-6.41	.002	-2.99	.003
-5.67	.004	-2.63	.012
-4.92	.003	-2.26	.019
-4.18	.002	-1.90	.023
-3.43	.002	-1.53	.047
-2.69	.008	-1.17	.061
-1.94	.030	-0.80	.076
-1.19	.099	-0.43	.103
-0.45	.113	-0.07	.115
0.30	.581	0.29	.179
1.04	.142	0.66	.176
1.79	.007	1.02	.099
2.54	.002	1.39	.050
3.28	.001	1.75	.022
4.03	0	2.12	.008
4.77	.001	2.48	.002
		2.85	.001
		3.21	.001

a Actual price minus the mean of prices divided by the standard deviation of prices.

Table B-6

PATTERNS OF GRADE OF GASOLINE REPORTED IN THE FOUR PRICE FIELDS IN THE LUNDBERG DATA

| | Grade in: | | | | | Number of |
Pattern	1st position	2nd position	3rd position	4th position		Stations
RP__	R	P	—	—		8,684
RMP_	R	M	P	—		6,347
RM__	R	M	—	—		74
SRP_	S	R	P	—		463
SRMP	S	R	M	P		19
SMP_	S	M	P	—		728
SP__	S	P	—	—	984	134
P___	P	—	—	—		122
All patterns						16,671

Note: R = regular grade; S = subregular grade; M = midgrade; P = premium grade; — = blank.